Praise for
Your Third Eye

"Misia Welters has expertly created a very unique and informative aid to understanding the Self. An especially useful tool for anyone who wishes to know more about true human capacity, depth, and consciousness."

—David Lambert, actor, writer, director

"This book is a portal to our vast and unexplored inner architecture. The magic and revelations that unfold through the practices that Misia reveals can offer profound connection to the grand universe, and thus, ourselves."

—Elinor Moshe, co-founder of Truth of You, co-host of *Resonant Truth*

"Misia has created the perfect grounded guide of exercises to increase your intuition and psychic skills, helping you become a sensible and sensitive person!"

—Pythian Priestess, founder of Pythian Mystery School

"Intuition is one of those forces we can never fully grasp, yet we can learn to navigate it, shape it, and recognize its language to scratch that existential itch. Misia has done a splendid job putting words to something most people can only feel. She brings clarity to a realm that usually escapes definition, offering a grounded path into a very mystical field. If you're ready to explore the deeper layers of your mind and reconnect with the intelligence that lives beyond logic, this book will guide you beautifully."

—Irah Morffi, metaphysician and entrepreneur

Your Third Eye

Your Third Eye

**Connecting Dream Science,
Intuition, and the Subconscious
to Finally See Yourself and the World**

by

MISIA WELTERS

MIAMI

Copyright © 2026 by Misia Welters.
Published by Key Lime Publishing, a division of Media Agency Services (MAS) LLC.

Cover, Layout & Design: Megan Werner
Cover Illustration: Anastasiia Hevko / stock.adobe.com
Interior Images: Misia Welters; Project Stargate files; Codex Atlanticus, folio 459r; Jacob Lee Adlington

No part of this book may be reproduced, stored in a retrieval system, or transmitted in any form or by any means—electronic, mechanical, photocopying, recording, or otherwise—without the prior written permission of the publisher, except in the case of brief quotations embodied in critical articles or reviews.

Key Lime Publishing supports authors' rights to free expression and artistic creativity. Copyright exists to encourage the creation of original works that enrich our culture and society. We ask readers to respect the intellectual property of our authors and to honor their work as you would your own.

For permission requests, please contact the publisher at:
Key Lime Publishing
5966 South Dixie Highway, Suite 300
Miami, FL 33143
info@keylimepublishing.com

For special orders, quantity sales, course adoptions and corporate sales, please email the publisher at orders@keylimepublishing.com.
For trade and wholesale sales, please contact Ingram Publisher Services at customer.service@ingramcontent.com or +1.800.509.4587.

Your Third Eye: Connecting Dream Science, Intuition, and the Subconscious to Finally See Yourself and the World

Library of Congress Cataloging-in-Publication Number: 2025946598
ISBN: (pb) 978-1-68481-873-0 (e) 978-1-68481-874-7
BISAC category code: OCC007000 BODY, MIND & SPIRIT / Psychic Phenomena / ESP

Printed in the United States of America

The information provided in this book is based on the research, insights, and experiences of the author. Every effort has been made to provide accurate and up-to-date information; however, neither the author nor the publisher warrants the information provided is free of factual error. This book is not intended to diagnose, treat, or cure any medical condition or disease, nor is it intended as a substitute for professional medical care. All matters regarding your health should be supervised by a qualified healthcare professional. The author and publisher disclaim all liability for any adverse effects arising out of or relating to the use or application of the information or advice provided in this book.

*To those that know that they are
capable of more.*

TABLE OF CONTENTS

Introduction 10

Chapter 1: How Do You Experience Impossible Things and Stay a Sensible Person? 16

Chapter 2: Intuition Affects You More Than You Know 27

Chapter 3: Ancient Wisdom and the Mystery of the Third Eye 50

Chapter 4: The DMT Conversation 62

Chapter 5: Dream States and the Mystery of 3:00 to 5:00 a.m. 92

Chapter 6: Women, Children, and Blindsight Phenomena 109

Chapter 7: The Creative Nature of Consciousness 124

Chapter 8: Intuition in Terms of Pattern Recognition 146

Chapter 9: How Meditation Enhances Intuition 170

Conclusion: Magic Exists 188

References 189

Acknowledgments 205

About the Author 207

Introduction

We are living in an age of possibility. We are more connected to each other than ever and have access to intelligent answers right at our fingertips through social media and new AI tools. But with access to so much intelligence and so many answers, are we really that much happier for it? In theory, we should be, right?

A survey of nearly 1,700 respondents reveals that nearly two-thirds of people aged sixteen to twenty-four believe social media does more harm than good.[1]

It feels like we are drowning in information but starving for wisdom. I believe that people are more disconnected from themselves now than ever before.

Through our minds' eyes everything comes into focus, yet we have so many places to put our awareness outside of ourselves that it's easy to get lost in a sea of meaningless information, unconsciously looking for the hit that will give us the clarity we desire when the answer that we are looking for is right where we are.

---

[1] "Generation Z Expresses Concerns Regarding the Toxicity and Addictiveness of Social Media," Disinformation Social Media Alliance, April 17, 2025, https://disa.org/generation-z-expresses-concerns-regarding-the-toxicity-and-addictiveness-of-social-media.

Without introspection, we would simply fall into the mould of our environment, pacified by the same answers to the same questions as passion slips through our fingers.

The rhythm of life is speeding up; the pace of change is becoming more and more rapid. Alan Watts believed we were living in the age of anxiety back in the sixties, that modern society's emphasis on materialism had caused a profound disconnect from the deeper, more meaningful aspects of existence.[2] Since the sixties, this emphasis on materialism has only increased, but the interesting thing is that more people seem to be becoming aware of it.

Consciously allowing space for your inner world is more important now than ever. Learning to tune into how you feel and listening to your intuition will be what helps you to swim through the noise with purpose.

When we become more open and familiar to those deeper layers of the mind, we find ourselves with greater clarity, inspiration, and direction. We also expand our awareness of the world around us.

You can be sitting in front of a fantastic lecturer with all the answers that will help you get to where you want to be, but are you aware? Are you listening? How well are you able to engage? They can be telling you precisely what you need to hear—while you put your awareness elsewhere, distracted in the back of your mind, because you are not conscious enough of those inner callings to know these are the words that will set you on the path that will feel good for you.

When you are disconnected from your inner world and intuition, you won't be able to connect to the cues that will help you move forward.

How well are you able to connect to these words? Perhaps as you read these words you feel a mix of emotions, phrases, or memories

---

2   Alan W. Watts, *The Wisdom of Insecurity: A Message for an Age of Anxiety* (Pantheon Books, 1951).

popping up in your mind's eye as you follow along? Or perhaps your awareness is well directed, and you can feel each black word on the page slice through your psyche to your core as you feel its meaning for you; or perhaps the words tap on the surface like raindrops on a window, while deeper down you are in the flow of questions that feel like they mean more to you at this moment.

The message that will take you where you want to be deep down can be shouted right at you. It can shake your shoulders and beg you to listen; but if you can't connect to it, if you are not aware of these deeper callings, it will be no good to you.

> *"Until you make the unconscious conscious, it will direct your life and you will call it fate."*
> — Carl Jung

When you know yourself deeply, you become more open to paths that lead to a life filled with a greater sense of meaning and fulfilment, and you become more receptive to the things that will lead to the change that you are perhaps craving.

The topic of intuition is one that is deeply misunderstood. Science has struggled to grasp it, and yet it is an undeniable part of what it means to be human. The nature of nonmaterial knowledge often seems to get brushed under the carpet in this modern era, one in which what can't be measured is seen as less valuable; but I believe that finding your own path and your own meaning is the most valuable thing of all and introspection should be more explored and encouraged. One present life lived with clarity in vision is a far richer and meaningful experience than two distracted ones sparsely following every outside calling.

I grew up very in tune to my inner world. I can say that with confidence as I have been meditating regularly from the age of twelve. It has been a very strange journey for me since I experienced a lot of intuitive phenomena very early. I grew up with family members who were familiar with mystical experiences like mine, but it was still very confusing to see how little people seemed to be open to my experiences outside of the gates of spiritualism. This always distressed me and made me question my experiences very deeply. It made me want to break free from the woo-woo box that I was pushed into. What I experienced was too real and too shocking, and with investigation of other people's experiences, things added up in a way that showed there was definitely something more than chance or collective delusion.

On the way, I have gained a new perspective on psychic phenomena and intuition that seems more grounded in understanding, one that I believe could help a lot of people grasp the power of their inner voice and how to hear it, trust it, and allow it to guide them.

Many of the ideas I explore in this book stem from ancient Eastern traditions such as Hinduism, Buddhism, and Taoism. I want to acknowledge that I wasn't born into those cultures. I grew up tuning into my inner world and navigating intuitive experiences; and in time, I found that the deeper truths I was experiencing were already explored in these ancient systems of thought, which is what drew me to them.

My intention isn't to claim any kind of ownership over these traditions; traditions should be honoured. There is so much intelligence in these philosophies; and the more that I learn, the more I am blown away by how certain truths are reflected in them—by how much awareness of the depths of their minds they must have had to reach certain conclusions.

The insights we find on the path inward are universal. They don't belong to one culture; they live in the human experience itself. My goal is to share what I've learned in a way that helps people who have experienced intuitive phenomena firsthand to feel less alone, more connected to their own truth, and more aware of the intelligence within them, wherever they're from and however they arrive at this path.

After reading this book, you will have explored many angles on the nature of intuition and consciousness, including scientific, philosophical, and spiritual perspectives. I want to give you the option to use this understanding of intuition to find *your own truth and meaning* through the empowerment of your inner wisdom so that you can live a rich life.

Being in tune with your intuition is not just helpful for the big existential questions in your life, it also helps you to feel more centred in your day-to-day to make all the little decisions that ultimately build up the big picture. Perhaps you might think of introspection and topics such as meditation as boring. Perhaps you have little patience or find that looking inward brings up feelings of anxiety or unease at first, like so many people today. But when you get a glimpse of what it really means to be present, to break through to altered states of consciousness and experience intuitive phenomena for yourself, it is nothing short of life-changing. It makes you realise how much power you really have to shift the narrative of your life.

I will go on to explore the interpretations and extent of inner knowing from a wide range of different angles, integrating observations of consciousness and timeless philosophical wisdom with a more grounded approach in psychology.

We will dive into great mysteries of the third eye and explore the purpose of DMT in the body, including its potential role in mystical experiences that occur in meditation, dream states, and near-death experiences. I believe that understanding the role of this highly potent psychedelic, which is naturally found in the human body, could help us better understand human consciousness in a few aspects.

Along with helping you to acquire a deep understanding of the nature of intuition and a basic understanding of how to navigate the language and deeper messages of the subconscious mind, I will teach practical methods of learning to connect to intuitive messages through dream states, meditation methods, and various other divination techniques curated from a wide range of esoteric traditions. Who knows, perhaps you will also experience phenomena along the way.

This book is about reclaiming the lost intelligence within, opening people up to the wonders of the mind, and helping those who have encountered mystical experiences to better understand them.

Just how far can the extent of inner knowing really go?

That's the golden question that I prompt us to ask. This is the question I have been chasing for as long as I can remember, one that has deeply shaped my path and taken me on a journey that many people would not believe.

Let's explore this question together.

Chapter 1

How Do You Experience Impossible Things and Stay a Sensible Person?

My childhood was unique. I had a heightened awareness of my intuition, and so, for a lot of my life, I have been facing the mystery of intuition head-on, trying to realise any kind of truth that could come from it. The extent of intuition has been a scientific mystery for as long as we have been around. Intuition is an inner knowing that goes beyond reason. Have you ever walked into a room full of people and been instantly struck by a strong and indescribable feeling that gives you insight into the overall mood of those present? Or perhaps you have experienced dreaming of a friend you haven't spoken to in years, and then the next day, they call you unexpectedly to share important news. That is your intuition speaking to you.

We like to say that as humans we are rational beings. We need reason to make everything make sense, otherwise it's just too stressful; but people often underestimate how much of life exists in the grey area and how much we rely on chance and loosely tied threads in our day-to-day lives.

When it comes to experiencing phenomena beyond the everyday, it's easier if you have some sort of faith; then you can just call it a miracle or divine intervention, and that is enough to be able to move forward without falling down into some sort of existential spiral.

Experiencing an intuitive phenomenon once, it is enough just to brush it under the carpet; twice is questionable, but experiencing impossible things regularly is when you either admit insanity, turn to religious thinking, or begin questioning what is really possible.

Growing Up Experiencing Intuitive Phenomena

When I was a kid, my friends and I made a joke about this strange sensitivity that I had. I remember us laughing about it and calling my intuition "tinglies." My childhood intuition was able to get us out of dangerous situations when we were playing on the street and helped me to guess with pinpoint accuracy the outcomes of certain situations in a way that always shocked people.

It got to a point where this sensitivity became so intense that I struggled to direct my awareness and was completely ungrounded, as my mind was picking up so much noise from my environment that it became unbearable.

Perhaps a regular household would have turned to a therapist or mental health specialist, but my mum reached out to a psychic family friend for insight on my state of heightened awareness. Her name is Cindy, and she worked with the police sometimes.

Mum would tell me about the stories Cindy would relate, and they were so fascinating. I remember my mum once told me that Cindy did a reading for a woman who was asking for guidance on her marriage: Cindy told the woman her husband was cheating and that he was with this other woman right at that moment, and if she was quick, she could catch him with her. The woman drove off, and sure enough, she caught him cheating.

Cindy told my mum that I had a "clairvoyant gift" and that if I kept up a meditation practice, I would have better control of this gift. I loved it, of course. If you tell a twelve or thirteen-year-old girl that she has some sort of psychic abilities that need to be maintained and better controlled by daily meditation, you bet that she will end up meditating every night.

My Early Experiences with Meditation

Like clockwork, every night before bed I would go onto YouTube, search up twenty-minute guided meditation recordings, and sit in a dark room with my legs crossed on the floor, listening closely to each track for direction.

Some days, my mind would be foggy, and it was difficult to connect to anything at all—as if my mind was rejecting the experience. On other days, however, I was able to connect to really deep states. These states were like nothing I had ever experienced before, and they excited me.

It's hard to explain just how it feels to think no thoughts and have your awareness completely immersed in your body, feeling every pump of your heart, the flow of your bloodstream, the gravity of your flesh, and the movement in your lungs simultaneously. It's especially difficult to describe to someone who has never experienced the unique and intense feelings that become available to you when you are able to direct and transform your awareness with focused control.

I then found meditations that exercised the imagination. I had a particularly vivid imagination as a child, something that was reflected in my dream states. My dreams were very vivid and often had complex storylines and imagery that seemed almost psychedelic, so I was pretty easily able to connect to meditations that exercised one's visualisation and imagination.

I started practicing meditations that took you through journeys into the mind and meditations encouraging the exploration of intuitive insight, which is the kind of insight that can be profound, but you are not quite sure where it came from.

Journeying is a meditation practice stemming from shamanic traditions in which you explore the inner world; you see what emerges when you go into deep states of introspection and then apply your imagination to give form to the deeper aspects of your mind.

Through these journeying meditations, I would walk through luscious forests, swim in streams. With enough time and later guidance, I eventually had my own mapped plot of land where I would go to retreat from the external world. (I sometimes go to this same space in my mind to this day.)

The more I practiced, the more vivid my experiences got—but they were not always linear. I found that as the states I was able to connect to deepened, the more abstract my experiences became. Sometimes I would get little surprises, visions or symbols that popped up—random intuitive insights and inner guidance that came to me.

These insights were often really quite profound, and it didn't feel as if they were coming from my rationally thinking mind because after meditating and listening to the insights, they would make me think and question them. But I followed their guidance, it never led me astray.

Going Deeper into Exploring Intuition in Meditations

I started practicing going into these meditations with a list full of questions, and sure enough, I got answers. In some of these questions, I asked about other people in my life, what different outcomes would look like for me if I followed certain paths, and how to achieve the things I wanted to achieve.

I went into meditations with no expectations, just the intention of exploring the extent of the psychic phenomena that were opening up to me.

Sure enough, the information that I could pick up kept turning out to be insightful and true in a way that went beyond reason.

Some things were shockingly true. One time, I randomly had a vision of my science teacher pregnant, and within a few months she shared with the class that she was going to have a child. What I experienced should have been impossible, but it happened. Not only did it happen, but this insight came to me in a controlled environment that I created.

Reading People

When I was around fourteen or fifteen years old, I decided to explore what I could pick up from other people. When I was bored in class at school, I would often focus on each person one at a time, and my imagination would trail off into fairly specific storylines. To explore the validity of whether what I was picking up or not was true, I sat with my friends in class one time and suggested we play a guessing game to see who got the most information about each other right.

It got to my turn, and, as I was used to doing in my meditations, I allowed space for my imagination.

"Do you have three cousins, two older boys and one younger girl?"

The girl that I was guessing about was shocked and got defensive, asking if I had looked up her family online. I didn't know how to react, so I just laughed awkwardly. Wow, that was pretty specific and random information.

So, What Now?

At this point I was on a mission: I wanted to test this strange phenomenon and learn as much as I could from it.

Along with a friend outside of school, whenever I would meet new people, I would tell them that I wanted to try something and do the same thing I described above. Usually, it was by the skate park, which was our hangout spot at the time.

I didn't speak about this kind of thing in school really. I wasn't that popular, and I didn't want to become the subject of cruel jokes about "the girl who thinks she is psychic." I knew how that sounded, and I would just melt if I was confronted by a crowd of people demanding that I show them. I wouldn't be able to do it in those circumstances; you have to be in a very calm mindset where your thoughts flow. I knew that I would not be able to compose myself in a way that I could show them under such pressure.

When I read people in person, it felt scary every time. I would just start talking without thinking, knowing the irrational nature of how I would assume whatever arose from my imagination to be a fact.

Some of the things were really deep, and other stuff was random. "Does your mum have a crazy obsession with pink wafers by any chance?" I asked one girl. "Yeah, she has a shelf just full of them," she replied with a confused look on her face and a smile.

There were a few experiences that really stuck with me, though, There were experiences so shocking that they cemented the strange reality I had somehow tapped into in a way that was actually quite stressful at the time, experiences that had me going back to my friends asking, "Did that really happen?" in case I had lost the plot and not realised it. I was always constantly aware of the absurdity of what I was experiencing.

My friends and I sometimes hung out in a big shed we found in the middle of some forest space. It was very run down; it had furniture with burn marks in the fabric, random sheets of corrugated metal on the ground, and empty cans of fizzy drinks everywhere.

I remember vividly it was summer. We were all sitting in the shed, and one of my friends said that they had invited a couple over—let's call them Bella and Mitch. Bella wanted me to see what I could pick up from her. I felt that something was bothering her, and I realised that what I had picked up was sensitive, so I took her to the side. I'd picked up on an argument between her aunt and her mum. I was able to pick up on details as specific as her aunt's lower back tattoo of a butterfly and her mum's short black hair. She was shocked. Her boyfriend came over and asked if I got it, and she nodded.

Another case that I remember there was this boy, very proud and not exactly the mystic type. I picked up some information, and it came across really strongly. I took him to the side and explained a scenario that I saw in my mind's eye. In this scenario, his dad kicked him out of the house in the middle of the night for playing music too loud. He laughed at me because he said that never happened. Weeks later when I was out with my friends, he approached us shouting. He was full of energy with wide eyes and kind of did a little skip jump on his way to speak to me. He told me that the exact night when I had picked up on that scenario, it played out exactly as I said it did.

I even had two sisters fall out because of me. I picked up some quite sensitive information about a girl's love life. There were two love interests; one was really tall with short hair and the other was short and slightly bigger around the waistline. She thought that her sister had told me and went shouting after her because she couldn't believe it.

I have many stories like this.

Things were becoming progressively more surreal. Every time I was able to pick up on such information, I was shocked, but with time it became my new normal. The kind of information that I could guess from people never really felt like solid information until I spoke it out loud and got confirmation; without the prompt to do so, it would have stayed a fragment of my imagination.

When I spoke to my family about it, my dad told me that he had actually experienced strange, intuitive moments his whole life. My mum later told me there had been moments that had scared her slightly when he had known exactly what she was thinking.

I also found out that many family members on my mum's side of the family had experienced psychic phenomena in dream states.

So now I had this impossible thing in my hands, I had tested it, explored its boundaries, and logged my experiences; and then it turned out that this impossible thing runs in my family and is actually far more commonly experienced than I had thought. This impossible thing definitely had become something, at least in my reality.

The Journey into Spirituality

Spiritual traditions seemed to be the only place that had any kind of answer for what I was experiencing. In the spiritual community, there seemed to be lots of people who had gone through things similar to what I had experienced, as well as many interpretations of what this ability was.

I started to do one-on-one sessions with a shaman specializing in psychic development. I was taught a wide range of techniques and tools following shamanic traditions and went on to use them in meditations for various goals, but mostly to open up to deeper intuitive insight and messages.

I also joined a psychic circle, a group of sensitive and intuitive people like myself who recognised the intelligence in meditation and wished to explore the possibilities of intuition. In these circles we would often read each other, and it was interesting to see how other people were able to pick up very detailed information from me too. I had never been read like that before, and it was reassuring to be read to such a specific degree by others.

In one session, we tried out automatic writing. This is a technique in which you begin by entering a very deep trance-like state, and then, with a sense of detachment from the pen in your hand, you "allow the subconscious mind to arise and take over" and write messages, drawing information from the other side. We would not be conscious of the words being written until after the meditation. After the meditation, I saw that there were seemingly random letters written on the page. I typed the letters into translation software, and sure enough, it turned out that I had written fluent sentences in perfect Polish. I am half Polish by blood but had never learned the language growing up. The sentences might have been very random, but they were perfectly coherent. They had the correct spelling and phrasing, and they had a consistent theme. I remember one being "put the eggs in the fridge" and another that was also kitchen-themed.

I was not born special; these experiences can be cultivated.

If I had not given my subconscious mind so much space or entertained the possibility of intuitive wisdom beyond logic with the support and understanding that I had, I would have likely never listened to those little whispers and subtle feelings, let alone taken them seriously or considered that they could possibly mean anything.

I might have dodged a bit of an existential rabbit hole if I had refused to pay attention to my intuition, but there is so much that I have learned on this path that I want to share. The mystery makes it magical, but my goal is and always has been to make these phenomena more tangible for people. Even if the shocking experiences that I have had might be a little beyond what can be believed (trust me, I understand), every single person has a subtle inner voice waiting for them to tune in and listen, one that can guide them in unimaginable ways.

I don't think that these experiences make me special. I think that I just *gave the possibility of these experiences space to breathe*. I am no "star child" or God-gifted person in some exceptional way this "gift" is often interpreted as requiring. This wisdom is for everyone, and the only thing holding all of us back is the knowledge and the trust to pursue meditations and listen to one's intuition. I think that we should all explore it and honour the hidden part of ourselves, an inner dimension that really can feel like magic in its highest form. Most people go their whole lives without exploring what their own mind is capable of.

I have been through a deep research journey to try and understand these experiences from many angles. Along the way, I have found some exciting discoveries which make the nature of inner wisdom and intuition more tangible. These are things that have helped me to understand myself better but also will help you to trust in your own inner voice and hopefully inspire you to tune in and listen to your intuition and act on it with confidence.

Learning to listen to your intuition is not just a fun party trick, it is life-changing. Being able to tune in to your intuitive insights helps in finding a sense of clarity, strengthening your connection with yourself, and the being able to see solutions in situations more easily.

So, how do you experience impossible things and stay a sensible person? In my case, it meant showing you the possibility of this impossible thing and guiding you to perhaps even experience it yourself. Let it enrich your life.

Chapter 2

Intuition Affects You More Than You Know

Intuition is not just about finding out shocking information about others or being able to read people well. Intuition is something that impacts you every day—how tuned in or tuned out you are to your intuition massively determines the quality of your life.

When you are in tune with your intuition, you view the world with a greater sense of clarity, and you also have more confidence in your decisions and a greater connection to what really inspires you. This kind of deep connection with yourself makes it easier to connect to a sense of meaning too. When you move through the world with that reassuring feeling of security in your inner compass, knowing that you can lean on it and trust it, life flows more. You become less stressed and feel more confidence in your ability to achieve things that are outside of your comfort zone.

The Role of Intuition in Everyday Decisions and Life Direction

One of the most common ways that your intuition affects you daily is in the process of decision-making. Every time that you make a decision, as you are crunching down to a conclusion, the nature of what guides your ultimate decision becomes more and more intuitive. This holds true from the smallest decisions, such as, "Should I have orange juice or apple juice with my breakfast?" to the biggest decisions: "Do I marry them or not?"

"Do I stay where I am, close to my family, or do I take a chance on my dreams and move far away for work?"

"Do I need to prioritise my rest or keep prioritising my work?"

Many people end up hung up on these big questions when they are disconnected from their intuition because they are uncertain. Even if they deeply crave change, where there is uncertainty, change can feel scary and unnatural.

Sylvia Plath wrote a beautiful and famous extract that really embodies this struggle of being unhappy where she is while also feeling paralysed by the question of which direction to step foot in. The main character in her book *The Bell Jar* describes herself sitting below a fig tree. Each fruit she saw represented a different future for herself.

"One fig was a husband and a happy home and children, and another fig was a famous poet, and another fig was a brilliant professor, and another fig was Ee Gee, the amazing editor, and another fig was Europe and Africa and South America…"[3]

At the end, she found she had waited too long to make a choice; the fruits went bad and dropped at her feet.

---

3   Sylvia Plath, *The Bell Jar* (Harper & Row, 1971).

This story is the perfect example of how uncertainty keeps you stuck waiting for the change that can only really be met when you find the confidence to act on your deeper desires—when you learn how to trust and act on your intuition even if you don't logically know what kind of path lies ahead of you. Without it, you are never going to make a decision and take action as a means to a greater goal that will bring you to a place of increased fulfilment.

Tragically, I see many people living out their lives very passively, feeling that same urge for change but without the patience to listen to their inner callings and the ability to trust their intuition. Years will pass, and they will still have that same feeling, the feeling of an itch that they haven't scratched or a longing that never goes away. This is the life that a lot of people accept for themselves because they are so disconnected from their inner self that they don't feel they can trust these gut feelings to guide them through the chaos that comes with change.

Dreams endlessly put off are the result of the inability to move through uncertainty.

When you are connected to your intuition, you will be able to step into the unknown with clarity, confidence, and trust, following that inner voice.

How Our Intuition Guides Us to See Order in the Chaos of Uncertainty

Uncertainty is what happens when you don't know exactly how to label what you feel about things. Our emotions hold keys to deeper callings—intuitive messages are more emotional than anything, these intuitive callings always start as a feeling.

When you listen to that deep sense of self-awareness, you are able to give form to those underlying emotions and come to a better understanding of them. You can therefore connect more to the deeper vision that acts as a guideline when it comes to stepping down any kind of new path.

In other words, when you are in tune with yourself and have clearer vision, you are able to foresee greater possibilities.

Stepping into the Unknown

I have noticed a quality that many successful people have is the ability to step into the unknown—to make a decision and take action even in uncertain situations. Those with this quality often believe in the idea of something greater to comfort them as they do so, whether that be the trust in a greater God in their favour, some sort of spiritual philosophy, a wiser guiding hand, or simply confidence in their vision.

The deeper we find a vision or insight within ourselves, the more meaningful and rewarding it feels when that vision is achieved or that insight is acted on. Some of the greatest creators, innovators, and artists have consciously used intuition or worked in ways that kept them in tune with their intuition.

How Great Minds in History Honoured the Power of Intuition

ALBERT EINSTEIN

Einstein might have been one of the best scientists in history, but he was actually quite the mystic. When it came down to coming up with his new ideas, he was very conscious about the importance of intuition and creativity even more so than logic, despite being celebrated as one of the top scientists in the world.

He wrote that intuition is the origin of all discovery and even called intuition "the only valuable thing."[4]

> "The Intellect has little to do on the road to discovery. There comes a leap in consciousness, call it intuition or what you will, and the solution comes to you and you don't know how or why" - Einstein

NIKOLA TESLA

Tesla also was highly intuitive. He came up with some of the greatest inventions, discoveries that are fundamental to modern technology. He was a visionary inventor, engineer, and physicist who laid the foundation for much of modern electrical engineering. He said that many of his ideas came to him in visions and unexplainable sudden flashes of insight. So, he would not piece together his ideas bit by bit, he supposedly just saw it all in one go.[5]

> "I do not think, I sense" - Tesla

Tesla often spoke about intuition. His approach was grounded in his ability to visualise concepts and ideas but also in his recognition

---

4 Albert Einstein, quoted in Evelyn Fox Keller, *A Feeling for the Organism: The Life and Work of Barbara McClintock* (W.H. Freeman, 1983).

5 Nikola Tesla, *My Inventions: The Autobiography of Nikola Tesla* (Electrical Experimenter, 1919).

of the importance of deeper, almost otherworldly insights that guided his work.

For Tesla, intuition was not a mysterious concept but an essential tool for innovation. His ability to access deep intuitive insights allowed him to think beyond conventional scientific limitations. He often spoke of having a "sixth sense" when it came to his inventions, a kind of hidden knowledge that could guide him to breakthroughs in a way that others couldn't replicate.

STEVE JOBS

Steve Jobs, the co-founder of Apple, often discussed the importance of intuition in his approach to product design and innovation. He believed that intuition played a crucial role in developing products that were both functional and aesthetically beautiful. He emphasized trusting your gut and following your intuition even when the path ahead seemed unclear.

So, how can we learn to connect to the deeper parts of our mind to access intuitive insight like these great minds in history?

The Relationship Between Intuition and the Sciences

While the concept of intuition has been around for thousands of years, science has always had an interesting and at times uneasy relationship with it due to the subjective nature of intuitive experiences. It's not exactly like we can put our minds under a scalpel to show exactly how we perceive things. It is in the deep perception or experience of our own psyche that intuitive phenomena happen. With time, however, we are getting closer to understanding what mystics have been tapping into for millennia.

Neuroscience today confirms that the unconscious mind processes massive amounts of information faster than conscious thought, and so when we come into subconscious experience, we end up in this reservoir of wisdom and highly intelligent insights that go beyond the intelligence of the surface conscious part of our mind.

Our mind processes around 11 million bits per second, yet our conscious mind only processes around 10–50 bits per second. Most actual mental processing happens outside conscious awareness.[6,7]

When I say coming into subconscious experience, this is something that could look like deep states of meditation, dream states, or even sometimes psychedelic experiences (a topic I will expand on later).

If awareness of the subconscious mind is key to breaking through to deeper wisdom and knowing, it makes sense that when the mystic in a state of meditation in a candlelit cave reaches for answers from the ether while gazing into her crystal ball, she becomes connected to a hidden source within. "How do you know this?" you ask. "I just felt it," she says.

Carl Jung

The mystic has been described by Carl Jung as someone who has a deep awareness of the subconscious mind, and Jung stated that all mystical experience is the experience of the subconscious mind. You might hear this and think that it demystifies the experience by putting it in more tangible terms, but when it comes to what lies beneath the

---

[6] Tor Nørretranders, *The User Illusion: Cutting Consciousness Down to Size* (Penguin Books, 1999).

[7] John A. Bargh and Tanya L. Chartrand, "The Unbearable Automaticity of Being," *American Psychologist* 54, no. 7 (1999): 462–479, https://doi.org/10.1037/0003-066X.54.7.462.

subconscious mind, things get far more mysterious. There is only so far that psychology or neurobiology can reach into the depths of the psyche before it becomes less a matter of science and more of a philosophical matter. The deeper into the mind, the deeper the mystery.

Carl Jung was a Swiss psychiatrist and psychoanalyst who lived from 1875 to 1961. He was one of the most influential thinkers in psychology, a pioneer who helped shape how we understand the human mind, particularly the unconscious.

Deep in our unconscious lies the collective unconscious. It's like a reservoir of shared knowledge deep within us—a universal, inherited part of the unconscious mind that contains archetypes, symbols, and knowledge common to all humans. Jung said in his book *Memories, Dreams, Reflections* that the future is unconsciously prepared long in advance, which is the reason why it could be tapped into by clairvoyants through the collective unconscious.[8]

Jung himself actually experienced a lot of "paranormal" psychic phenomena throughout the course of his life and spent a good portion of it trying to understand it.

A few of his stories really stick out to me.

Carl Jung's Cases of Psychic and Intuitive Phenomena

Once Jung was awakened by a dull pain in the back of the head, feeling as though something had passed through his forehead and into the back of his skull, and he got the impression that someone had come into the room. When he turned on the light, however, no one else was in the room. The following day, he received a telegram saying that his patient had committed suicide by shooting himself in the head.

---

[8] Carl G. Jung, *Memories, Dreams, Reflections*, ed. Aniela Jaffé, trans. Richard and Clara Winston (Pantheon Books, 1963).

Another time, at a wedding, he was seated across from a man he didn't know and began telling a "made-up" story during their conversation about criminal psychology. As he spoke, the man's expression changed and the atmosphere at the table grew tense. Embarrassed, Jung stopped talking; he later found out from another guest that the story he had told was actually the true life story of the man across from him down to every detail.

He had a series of prophetic dreams in 1913 depicting Europe engulfed in a sea of blood. These visions occurred months before the outbreak of World War I.

Jung later discovered that other intellectuals and spiritual leaders had reported similar premonitions, reinforcing his belief in a collective unconscious that could manifest insights during times of impending crisis.

The Process of Transmuting Subconscious Insight to Form

When we become still, particularly in meditative states, we find a greater sense of clarity and uncover more form in the at first intangible and chaotic fog of feeling, which is where hidden insights lie.

I have given a lot of thought to how I experience this; it is almost a kind of translation of deeper feelings into more intuitive information when I am consciously looking for answers in meditation. I have noticed that it always starts as a state of chaos and uncertainty, then a feeling arises; as I focus on that feeling more, it begins to find more form, and then I see things symbolically, flashes of ideas and visions without much form. After that, with enough attention and time, as I continue to focus on these thoughts, words, sentences, information, and answers to whatever it is that I have been reflecting on emerge.

I would say that the shock factor of the level of insight that you bring to light through this process comes from the level of depth at which you are able to meet yourself. The longer that you are able to stay with a meditation practice, the deeper that you are able to go.

I started viewing the mind like a mandala: At the very centre is pure consciousness, then we have the collective unconscious, the unconscious mind, and the conscious mind as we move toward the outer edge, and then on the outer layer would be our persona. I made this diagram to help me to better visualise this way of understanding the psyche.

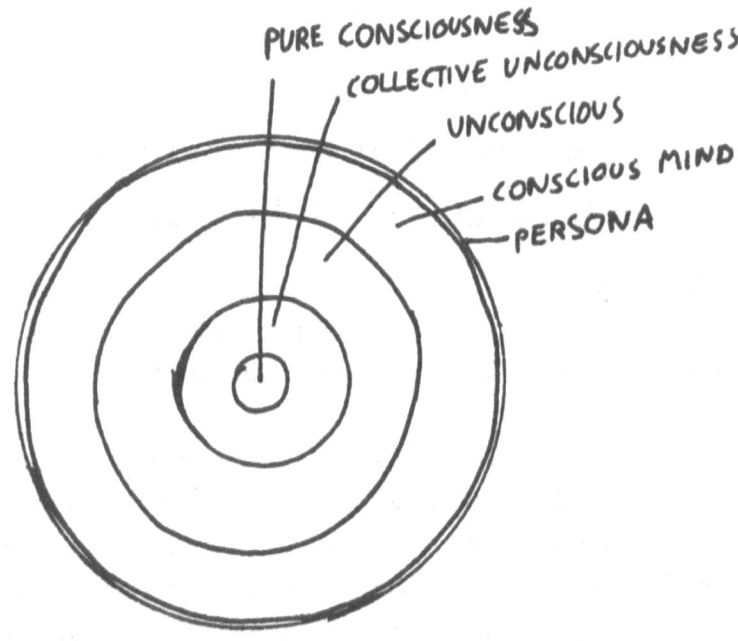

In meditation, we penetrate these layers of the mind as we come closer to pure consciousness. As we do so, the nature of our thoughts becomes more formless. Your ability to sit with the uncertainty of this feeling determines your ability to transmute it to form and find order in the chaos of your emotions so that you can succeed in bringing subconscious wisdom to light.

> "My brain is only a receiver, in the universe there is a core from which we obtain knowledge, strength and inspiration. I have not penetrated into the secrets of this core but I know that it exists."
> — Nikola Tesla

Jung also believed that the psyche had a nature that could be mapped to a mandala or that the essence of the mandala had significant importance in our quest to understand ourselves deeply.

I found out that for a period of his life, Jung would draw mandalas every morning as a way to observe the process of his psychic transformations and that he also got his patients to draw them too. He described them as "cryptograms concerning his state of self" and said that it became increasingly clear to him that the mandala was the "centre." He would interpret his own mental state and that of his patients through the mandala, which I have personally have since taken to as an activity to slow down and evaluate my own present state. I'd recommend it!

I also find it interesting that the idea of coming to the centre as a conscious act is something which is reflected in many Eastern philosophies. Some religions say that you meet God at your centre, which is very interesting considering that many religions say that you should go into meditation with the intention of consulting God for answers since the more subconscious aspects of the mind hold deeper wisdom.

In *Memories, Dreams, Reflections*, Jung said:[9]

> "I began to understand that the goal of psychic development is the self. There is no linear evolution, there is only circumbulation of the self, uniform development exists, at most, only at the beginning; later everything points towards the centre"
> – Jung

Here he states that in order to be aligned with yourself deeply, you must journey to the centre of your being.

I find this very interesting as in several ancient spiritual philosophies, mandala-like shapes are very important and hold a great deal of deeper meaning, for example:

- Hinduism
- Buddhism
- Jainism
- Christianity
- Taoism
- Native American traditions

In Hinduism and Buddhism, they make use of particular kinds of mandalas called yantras, which are different geometric shapes that are meditated on to reach different states of mind: a technique I find extremely interesting considering Jung's views on mandalas.

> "Stay in the centre and you will be able to move in any direction"
> – Alan Watts [10]

---

9   Carl G. Jung, *Memories, Dreams, Reflections*, ed. Aniela Jaffé, trans. Richard and Clara Winston (Pantheon Books, 1963).

10 Alan W. Watts, *The Way of Zen* (Pantheon Books, 1957).

Making a "journey to find the centre" might sound quite abstract and confusing at first, but it's actually simpler than that when you break it down. Slow down enough to come back to yourself. Let yourself become familiar with your uncertainty, sit with your emotions, and you will come to break through to a deeper level of intuition and inner guidance when you need it.

Symbolism and the Subconscious

"The soul never thinks without a picture"
— Aristotle [11]

Let's return to the image of the mystic gazing into the crystal ball and speaking deep insights. Mystics often talk in very symbolic terms, and symbolism is found across ancient cultures and religions.

So why is this?

The language of our subconscious mind is symbolic.

Symbols are objects of the known world hinting at something unknown: It is the known expressing the life and sense of the inexpressible. Symbols have an indescribable quality; they resonate with our minds in a way that words can't quite reach, in an indescribable resonance that comes *before* words, or even a more intuitive language.

To illustrate how the symbol comes before language in a practical way, consider the "kiki" and "bouba" effect. Take a look at the diagram below; which one would you label "kiki" and which one would you label "bouba?"

---

[11] Aristotle, *On the Soul (De Anima)*, trans. J. A. Smith and W. D. Ross (Clarendon Press, 1908).

The "kiki" and "bouba" effect was demonstrated when kids as young as two-and-a-half identified the rounder symbol as "bouba" and the spiky symbol as "kiki."[12] These are seemingly meaningless shapes, along with seemingly meaningless words, and yet there is an intuitive resonance—an indescribable feeling that ties these images together.

This is why I believe that symbols come before language in our psyche when translating emotions. More complex emotions are more easily described through images and symbols than through language, especially in our deepest states of mind, where the nature of our experiences becomes harder to describe.

Neuroscientific research shows that the insula and amygdala (brain regions tied to emotional awareness) are active during intuitive decision-making.[13] Intuition is not "just a feeling," but feelings are often how intuition communicates.

When I have experienced intuitive insight, it kind of first starts as a flash vision that I experience emotionally. When I used to read people one-on-one in person, I remember the feeling would always come first and then I would get flashes of vision packed with symbols and scenes.

[12] Daphne Maurer et al., "The Shape of Boubas: Sound-Shape Correspondences in Toddlers and Adults," *Developmental Science* 9, no. 3 (2006): 316–322, https://doi.org/10.1111/j.1467-7687.2006.00495.x.

[13] X. Gu, et al., "Anterior Insular Cortex and Emotional Awareness," *Journal of Comparative Neurology* 521, no. 15 (2013): 3371–3388, https://doi.org/10.1002/cne.23568.

A lot of the time they wouldn't necessarily make sense to me, but when I communicated these visions with the person I was reading, the details of the visions often struck a very deep resonance with them.

Often symbols have far deeper meaning and wisdom than we can connect to immediately. We can frequently keep returning to the same symbol again and again, each time arriving at deeper truths.

Have you ever wondered why across world religion and ancient spiritual philosophy, the same symbols show up despite there having been no modern means of communication?

What if I told you that deep in our unconscious, we have a shared reservoir of knowledge that can only be consciously perceived in our absolute deepest states, where the depths we can reach are yet unknown? The collective unconscious is the Jungian concept I shared with you earlier in this chapter.

Here for example is a geometric shape that shows up in places of worship across the world otherwise known as the "Flower of Life":

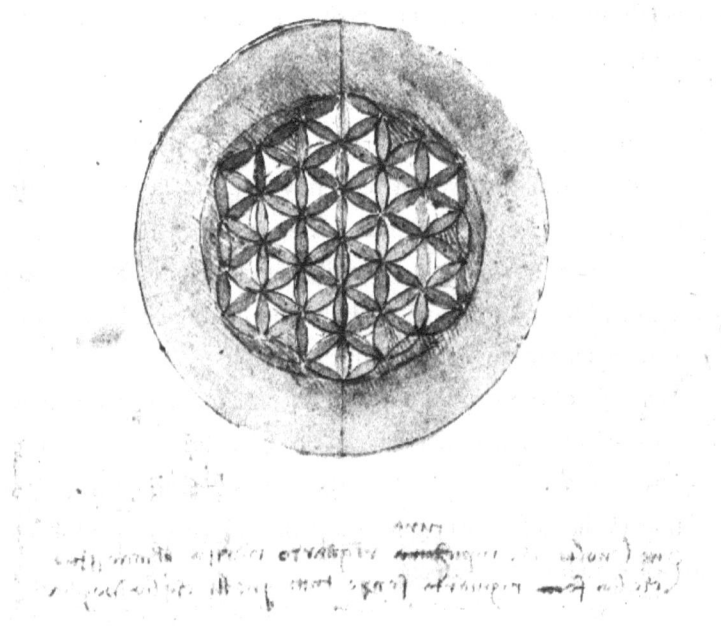

One of the oldest known examples of the Flower of Life is found in the Temple of Osiris in Egypt, which is estimated to be at least six thousand years old (though some argue it dates to the second century CE). The Flower of Life is found in diverse traditions, from Egyptian temples to Buddhist and Hindu yantras, Christian mosaics, and Native American designs.

This symbol is believed to have deeply metaphysical significance, as do many other forms of archetypal symbolism ("archetypal" meaning symbols experienced by all). The nature of symbolism in itself holds wisdom, and religions are particularly introspective aspects of all cultures, so it would make sense that these symbols tend to manifest the most often in religious and spiritual cultures. This is because their meditative practices psychologically enable deeper connection with the subconscious.

The way that this symbol shows up in so many places in ancient history only further affirms the existence of a deeper, more innate symbolism found in the depths of our psyche.

The CIA Experiments

This model or diagram that I created also reflects something I saw in the Stargate files.[14]

Stargate Project was a top-secret project exploring psychic and paranormal phenomena funded by the CIA that ended up being declassified in the nineties.

The CIA was studying things like astral projection and remote viewing, which is the ability to perceive information or even view through your mind's eye a distant location or event without physical access to or previous knowledge of this location. The project, which ran for over two decades, aimed to develop remote viewing as an intelligence-gathering tool.

The program involved various research and testing phases, including training individuals in remote viewing techniques, conducting experiments to assess their abilities, and attempting to apply these abilities

---

14   Central Intelligence Agency, *Analysis and Assessment of Gateway Process*, Wayne M. McDonnell. CIA-RDP96-00788R001700210016-5, Fort Meade, MD: US Army Operational Group, 1983. Online PDF, https://www.cia.gov/readingroom/docs/CIA-RDP96-00788R001700210016-5.pdf.

to intelligence gathering. Here are some of the tests straight from the files, including the viewer's description and a photo of the actual location.

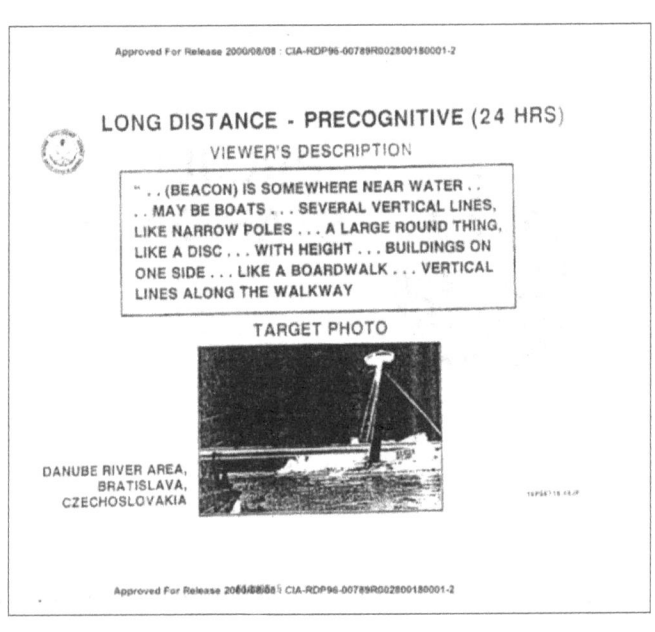

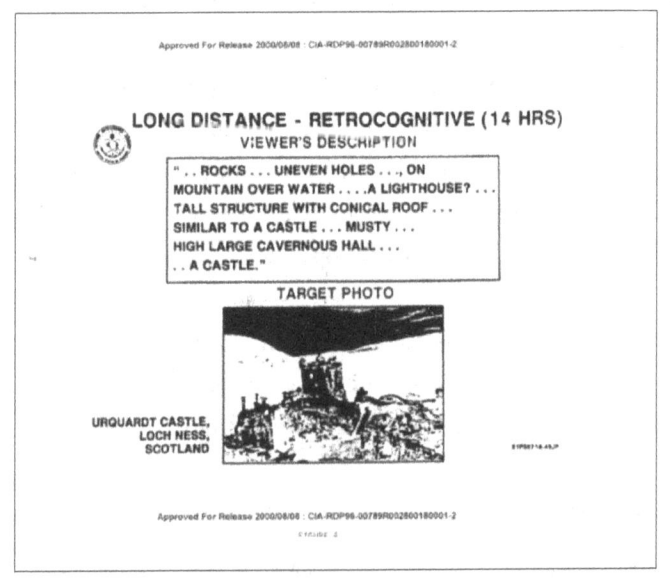

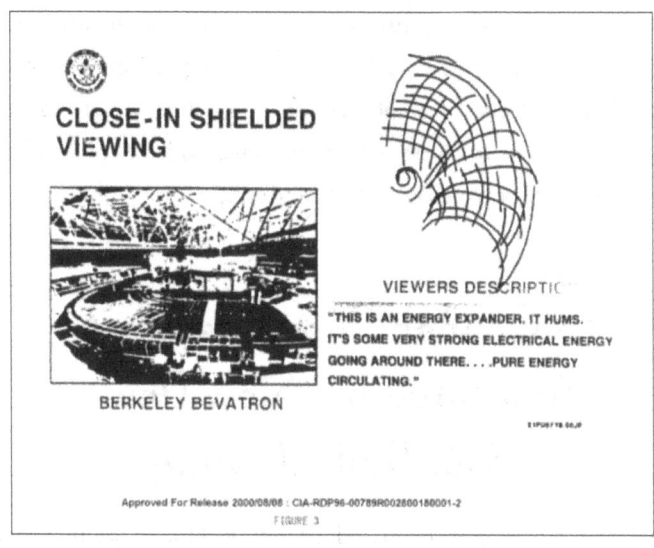

The viewer descriptions are pretty accurate, don't you agree? And now below is another mandala-like model of consciousness, one that reminded me a lot of my own:

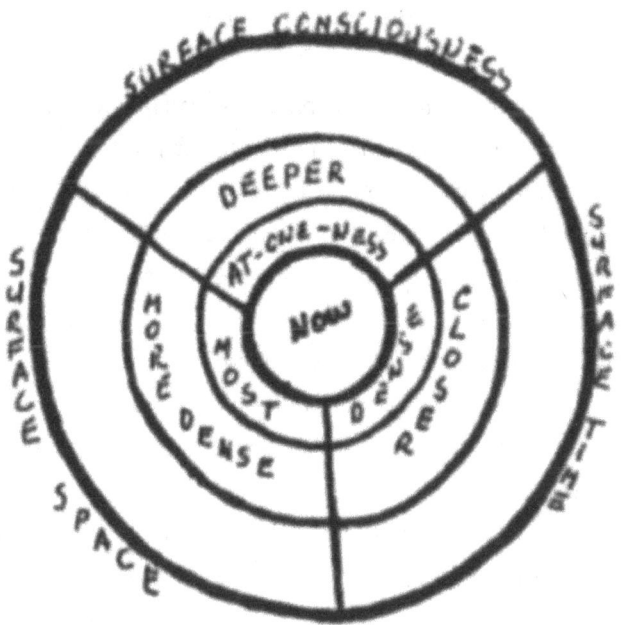

The text describes "surface time" as a human-constructed measurement of the past and future from the perspective of the present, suggesting that deeper levels of consciousness compress past and future into a unified "now." Researchers investigated how consciousness might influence perceptions of time and space.

To Connect More Deeply to Your Intuition, Slow Down Your Daily Routine

Now that you have more of an understanding of the profound benefits of a good connection with the deeper aspects of your mind, you may be wondering: How is this possible?

It's a lot simpler than you think.

Slow down.

Slow down your mind and allow time in your day-to-day for mind space.

There are many grounding practices available to improve self-connection, but I believe that in order to get you to a place where you are generally more grounded, there are small lifestyle changes that could benefit you greatly and help ease you into the right state of mind: a state that will make practices such as meditation not only more effective but easier as well.

Sustainable longer-term results come from small shifts in your daily routine, practiced regularly. If you can keep to them, making little changes will do more good than doing one long meditation once in a while.

When starting out with mindful practices, it is so important to work with yourself and your own habits. You need to know yourself well enough to know what is attainable for you. If you push yourself too far right away, you may find that you will want to reject the practice. If you are used to a fast-paced lifestyle and mindset and push yourself into a one-hour meditation right away, you are more likely to have an uncomfortable experience and end up rejecting the practice all together.

For those who are just getting started in practicing bringing presence into their lives or who have intentions of integrating a meditation practice into their everyday routines, here are some small things that you can do day-to-day that will help you to become more in tune generally.

Changing Your Media Habits to Enhance Intuitive Function

Different forms of media engage the mind in different ways. Some we can consume very passively, but with others we need to slow down enough to get more into their flow. Slower-paced media is significantly healthier for your brain and better for you if your long-term goal is being more in tune with your intuition.

For example, switching out a regular habit of scrolling fifteen-second video clips for ages to watching one longer video will help you to slow down.

Here is my rule of thumb for whenever I find myself wanting to make shifts in my media consumption:

- Move from viewing social media shorts to longer videos
- Longer videos to movies or documentaries
- Movies to audiobooks
- Audiobooks to books

If you were to take a moment to see how you feel after scrolling on social media for fifteen minutes vs. reading a book for fifteen minutes, the chances are that you are going to feel a lot better after reading a book, so it's worth making these changes your new habits.

When trying to be more present, the act of slowing down can be difficult as you end up facing the emotions that you have repressed, but by doing so, you come to a greater understanding of yourself.

Journaling

Something that helps me to sit with my emotions more and helps keep me present day-to-day is journaling. Every night my final ritual is to light a candle and sip a peppermint tea in bed with my diary to decompress, and I always feel lighter afterwards.

Journaling is a gentle way to process your thoughts and give form to your ideas. The act of journaling helps you to find a sense of clarity through all that you are experiencing, process and organize your thoughts, and make sense of the haze of emotions that might otherwise never be consciously acknowledged.

If you are new to the idea of journaling, here are some prompts to explore and write about.

Journal Prompts for Inner Connection

- What helps me feel most at peace?
- What part of me have I been ignoring or quieting down?
- What emotion is most present in me today, and what might be underneath it?
- What have I been trying to "fix" about myself that might instead just need love or understanding?

- If I let go of judgment right now, what truth would rise to the surface?
- What question keeps returning to me?
- What are three things I am grateful for at this moment?
- When do I feel most alive and connected to who I am?
- What habits or thoughts keep me disconnected from my true self?
- How do I typically react when I feel stressed or overwhelmed?

Chapter 3

Ancient Wisdom and the Mystery of the Third Eye

The more I leaned into trying to understand the nature of the intuitive mind, the more that I started to see how deeply this kind of understanding is found in religion and ancient schools of thought.

Many religions and other ancient spiritual cultural traditions support the development of the intuitive mind very well, whether consciously or unconsciously. Not only do they support the development of the intuitive mind, but many ancient rituals engage with the subconscious for particular outcomes. The idea of manifestation is a great example of this.

These ideas have been upheld by these traditions for thousands of years, yet today we are still revealing the relevance of the deep wisdom of the ancients to modern ways of thinking in many aspects.

How Science Has Caught up to Ancient Wisdom

Mantras

Ancient Intuition

Mantras have their earliest documented origins in the Vedic traditions of ancient India, dating back over three thousand years. A mantra is a word or phrase that is repeated during meditation or prayer to aid concentration, focus the mind, and invoke the metaphysical power of the chosen intention behind the phrase or sound. Mantras are often used to manifest certain outcomes in your life; for example, if you want to invite joy into your life, you might choose to repeat "I have joy in my life" over and over in a state of meditation. The phrase "I have joy in my life" would be your mantra in this example.

Modern Scientific Understanding

It is shown from a neuroscience perspective that repeating a mantra with intention can reduce stress, enhance focus, and essentially aid in rewiring the brain, ultimately opening us up emotionally to whatever intention is being affirmed via repetition, utilising neuroplasticity. Repetition rewires the brain.[15]

---

15 Aviva Berkovich-Ohana, et al., "Repetitive Speech Elicits Widespread Deactivation in the Human Cortex: The 'Mantra' Effect?," *Brain and Behavior* 5, no. 7 (July 2015): e00346, https://doi.org/10.1002/brb3.346.

The Power of Vibration

Ancient Intuition

The power of vibration, especially sound vibration, is one of the most ancient and universal spiritual concepts. It has surfaced in different ways in various religions and ancient schools of thought. Different energies are seen as associated with different frequencies in Eastern spirituality; sound vibration is consciously utilised in Buddhism through chants and drums to manifest certain purposes. The principles of Hermetic philosophy, the origins of which date back to a time around 200 BCE to 400 CE, strongly imply that the universe is vibrational. A more modern Hermetic text called *The Kybalion* published in 1908 states that all is vibration.[16]

Modern Scientific Understanding

We now understand scientifically from a quantum perspective that vibration is at the basis of all that exists. At a subatomic level, everything, including what feels solid, is made up of particles like electrons and protons. But these particles aren't just little dots of matter; they also behave like waves, which means that at the most fundamental level, matter is not fixed—it vibrates.[17]

---

[16] The Three Initiates, *The Kybalion: A Study of the Hermetic Philosophy of Ancient Egypt and Greece* (Yogi Publication Society, 1908).

[17] Jan Westerhoff, "Reality: Is Matter Real?," *New Scientist*, September 26, 2012, https://www.newscientist.com/article/mg21528840-700-reality-is-matter-real.

The Geometric Properties of Vibration

Ancient Intuition

I watched a video where Gregg Braden spoke about his trip to a Tibetan Buddhist monastery.[18] He was remarking at the mandalas on the walls, and one of the monks told him that they contained a secret within them.

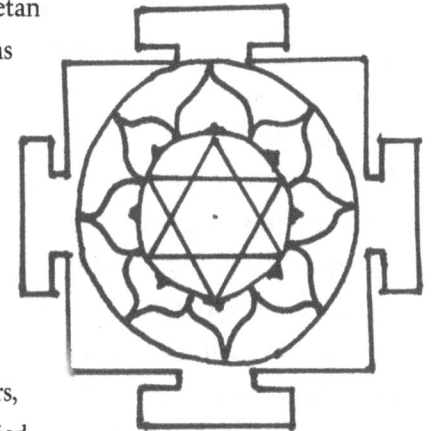

All those thousands of years ago they did not have the technology to record their sacred sounds—the prayers, mantras, and chants that carried the sounds of their ancestors. Instead, they would put them on the walls as yantras.

Modern Scientific Understanding

Today, cymatics, the science of visible sound, shows us that sound is not just heard; it's formative. Through cymatics we can see that when sound frequencies pass through a medium like sand, water, or air, they organize matter into geometric and mandala-like patterns that almost identically mirror many ancient mandalas and yantras.[19]

---

18 *Sound of Creation*, season 1, episode 1. "Sacred Secrets of Sound." Featuring Gregg Braden, released 2022, on Gaia. https://www.gaia.com/video/sacred-secrets-of-sound.

19 Hans Jenny, *Cymatics: A Study of Wave Phenomena and Vibration*, vol. 1 (MACROmedia Publishing, 2001).

There are many synchronicities like this; my point in pointing these out is that when science or "logic" would have otherwise called these impossible or irrational conclusions, there already was a collective shared method of coming to some advanced conclusions intuitively. All of a sudden science catches up to one of these conclusions and it becomes a "coincidence" or "phenomenon." Many of these are considered ancient mysteries, but it's no mystery to me.

Thousands of years have passed, and we are still finding our own language for the same truths that were originally reached intuitively long before. I now believe that religion and spiritual philosophy are inherently intuitive. While science relies on the logical mind to arrive at truths, spirituality relies on intuitive connection and metaphysical conclusions.

Now, as science catches up to wise ancient insights, we can see that there is not only one way of knowing. Every time science liberates ancient wisdom, I believe that it's less of a testament to the religion or spiritual agenda and more a testament to the extent that the intuitive mind can find truth without strict logic.

How Modern Life Disconnects Us from Intuition vs. How Ancient Lifestyles Supported It

I believe that many cultures in history were significantly more in tune with their intuition than we are today. It makes a lot of sense: People led far simpler lives with far fewer distractions. With social media, we now have the option to easily escape how we feel in a stream of fast-paced media consumption. It's easy to lose connection to the subtle whispers of subconscious wisdom or inner callings when curated distraction is so easily accessible.

The "fastest" media that people had in history were books, if they were lucky enough to be able to read, and perhaps the occasional play. Naturally, they would have had to face themselves more.

Other Ways Intuitive Intelligence Manifests in Ancient History

The more I look back into history, the more that it's clear to me that the ancients were on another level when it came to intuitive intelligence. People used to be able to memorise scriptures and poems thousands of lines long, and these were passed down orally. The *Rigveda*, for example, a foundational Hindu text, was passed down orally for over a thousand years with astonishing accuracy. This level of memorisation requires significant mental discipline, pattern recognition, and deep intuitive immersion. They could also track stars without telescopes, read subtle signs in nature, and accomplish navigation without maps or compasses.

While I'm not saying everyone in ancient times lived in some constant mystical state, I think the conditions of life back then were far more supportive of inner connection compared to the overstimulated, hyper-distracting culture we live in today.

They lived with far more presence. There were fewer distractions, as well as more simplicity and more rhythm—things that naturally bring us closer to ourselves. The nature and pace of media have definitely changed how we engage with our own minds. I believe that there is a lot that we can learn from the ancients.

Third Eye Symbolism in History

Returning to the shared symbolism in religion described in the previous chapter, I was particularly struck by the shared symbolism and definition of something called the third eye. Many cultures seemed to have some sort of common understanding of this concept that has been lost in the larger context of things.

I first got drawn to this mystery when I was a young teenager on the internet. I had seen many funky art pieces and spiritual cartoons of people with a third eye in the centre of the forehead, often paired with a caption affirming some sort of intuitive authority. Naturally, with the experiences that I had grown up with, seeing these made me want to do a little investigation. Could this really be a thing?

The Third Eye in Hinduism

In Hinduism, one of the gods, Lord Shiva, is known to be depicted with three eyes.

Shiva is the god of destruction and regeneration and master of poison and medicine. His right eye is considered the sun, his left eye the moon, and his third eye, located between his eyebrows, is the eye of spiritual wisdom and knowledge. It is believed that he uses his third eye to see beyond the apparent and protect good people from evildoers. There is a story about Shiva and how he opened his third eye to protect himself from the actions of Kama, the Hindu god of lust and love. The story goes that Kama shot an arrow through Shiva's heart; Shiva opened his third eye, and it burnt Kama to ashes.

Awakening the third eye is often a goal in yogic and tantric practices. It is said that when you have an awakened third eye, it enables you to see beyond illusion through to the true nature of reality. The third eye in Hinduism also represents the "inner fire" of consciousness that burns through ignorance.

Buddhism and Hinduism: Shared Beliefs

Both Hinduism and Buddhism share a belief in chakras. Chakras are energy centres in the body.

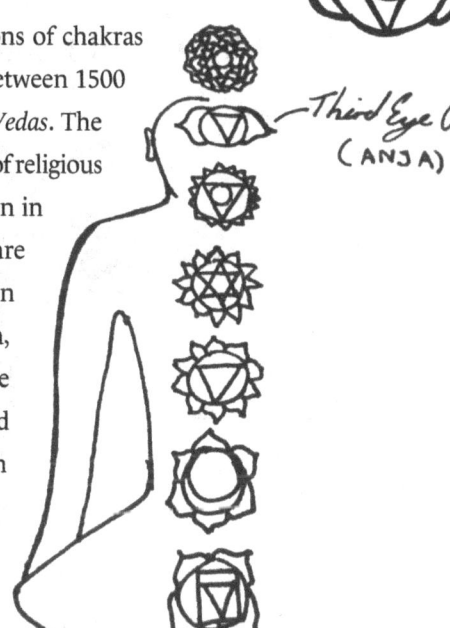

Third Eye Chakra: (ANJA)

The first mentions of chakras are found in India between 1500 and 500 BCE in the *Vedas*. The *Vedas* are a collection of religious texts originally written in Vedic Sanskrit; they are the oldest scriptures in Hinduism. The chakra, or energy centre, on the forehead is the third eye chakra. In both religions, you focus on this energy centre if you want to tap into these abilities:

- Intuition
- Inner vision
- Imagination
- Insight
- Mental clarity
- Discernment
- Self-reflection
- Connection to inner wisdom
- Perception of truth beyond illusion (a.k.a. "Maya")
- Clairvoyance/psychic vision
- Access to higher consciousness
- Awareness of archetypes and symbolic meanings

The Third Eye in Buddhism

More specifically, the third eye is called the "eye of consciousness" in Buddhism. It represents Buddha's awakened perspective or "eye of wisdom" that sees beyond mundane reality. Rather than it being depicted as an actual eye, in Buddhism, it is represented by a spiral dot on Buddha's brow called the *urna*. In traditional iconography, the *urna* between the eyebrows marks the Buddha's enlightened mind and reminds practitioners of insight and compassion.

The Eye of Horus in Ancient Egypt

The Eye of Horus is a symbol in ancient Egyptian religion that has links to the pineal gland. It has been called the "Eye of Truth (or Insight)", and the "Eye of God" inside the human mind. Sharing similarities with both Hindu and Buddhist ideas, the Eye gives insight into the immaterial world.

The Eye of Horus was seen as a sign of prosperity and protection that derived from the myth of Isis and Osiris. The sacred story of this myth started when Set, Osiris' brother, murdered Osiris to claim the throne. He then cut Osiris's body into fourteen parts and distributed them across ancient Egypt. Isis, Nephthys, Anubis, and Horus (all Egyptian gods) were able to find thirteen parts of Osiris' body so that he was able to pass onto the underworld. (You needed to be appropriately embalmed in order to pass onto the underworld in the religion of ancient Egypt at this time.) Horus killed Set, thereby restoring order to Egypt. Afterwards, Horus was idolized by the ancient Egyptians, including in the form of the Eye of Horus itself.

pineal gland (AKA 3ʳᴰ EYE)

corpus callosum

Thalamus

Western and Scientific Interpretations of the Third Eye: The Pineal Gland

Did you know that we have a third eye? Physically, in our bodies?

I found out that right at the very centre of the brain between the right and left hemisphere, you will find the pineal gland, otherwise known as the third eye. It is a pea-shaped gland made from eye tissue and shaped a little bit like a pinecone, which is where it got its name.[20]

Some have compared the location of the pineal gland in the brain with how the Eye of Horus looks in ancient Egyptian artistic renderings; I found it interesting that the positioning of the third eye in Buddhist and Hindu cultures was also exactly located on the forehead, near where the pineal gland would lie in the brain.

Descartes and the Pineal Gland

René Descartes, a French philosopher, mathematician, and scientist widely regarded as one of the founding figures of modern Western philosophy, believed that the pineal gland was the house of consciousness in the human body and that it was where thoughts formed. Descartes reasoned that the pineal gland is singular (unlike most brain structures, which come in pairs), making it, in his view, a suitable "centre" for the indivisible soul.

---

20 Richard J. Wurtman and Julius Axelrod, "The Pineal Gland," *Scientific American* 213, no. 1 (1965): 50–63, https://www.jstor.org/stable/24931939.

The pineal gland is also centrally located in the brain; Descartes famously said it had the "best seat in the house."[21]

Could this little gland really hold the key to understanding intuitive mystical experiences and the altered states of awareness that so many practitioners, including myself, have experienced in meditation? It seems pretty obvious that the ancients were implying something along those lines. The synchronicities and phenomena of these specific and similar ideas forming independently so many times makes them at least something worthy of attention.

How the Pineal Gland Is Understood by Science

The pineal gland's full purpose has never been fully understood by science, but we know for sure that it produces melatonin, which aids us in sleep.[22] Our pineal gland also sets our circadian rhythm, which acts as our body clock for things like releases of hormones, when to eat, when to sleep, and so on.[23]

With everything considered, surely you would assume it must do a little more than that?

I dug a little further and found something that would surely send me down one of the most interesting rabbit holes in my life: DMT.

---

[21] Gert-Jan Lokhorst, "Descartes and the Pineal Gland," *The Stanford Encyclopedia of Philosophy* Winter 2021 Edition (2021): https://plato.stanford.edu/archives/win2021/entries/pineal-gland.

[22] Josephine Arendt and Anna Aulinas, "Physiology of the Pineal Gland and Melatonin," in *Endotext*, ed. K. R. Feingold, S. F. Ahmed, B. Anawalt, et al. (MDText.com, Inc., 2000–), updated October 30, 2022, https://www.ncbi.nlm.nih.gov/books/NBK550972.

[23] Valér Csernus and Béla Mess, "Biorhythms and Pineal Gland," *Neuroendocrinology Letters* 24, no. 6 (2003): 404–411, https://pubmed.ncbi.nlm.nih.gov/15073565.

Chapter 4

The DMT Conversation

Disclaimer: Before I get started on this chapter, I feel the need to give a little disclaimer. Although I once tried a very low dose of truffles in Amsterdam, I do not use or promote the recreational use of psychedelics. My interest is purely in understanding consciousness and the cause of naturally occurring mystical states through meditation. My research on psychedelia has only deepened my reverence for natural insight.

The Realisation

When I first found out about the possibility of DMT being produced in the pineal gland, I was a teenager still living with my parents.[24] It was four in the morning, and I was so excited that I woke them both up.

Many of the things that I had already experienced, such as intuitive phenomena and even out-of-body experiences in meditation, are

---

24 Rick Strassman, *DMT: The Spirit Molecule: A Doctor's Revolutionary Research into the Biology of Near-Death and Mystical Experiences* (Park Street Press, 2001).

possibilities foreign to many people; but when I dug more into the psychological effects psychedelics have on people, I realised that there were shocking parallels. These effects, together with discoveries about the pineal gland and the fact that many spiritual practices depict psychedelic side effects as a possible result of meditation, completely fascinated me.

I had always been curious before about why it is that both meditation practitioners and psychonauts follow such similar schools of thought. Why is it that psychedelics have been used in spiritual practices with the belief that they connect you with some higher knowing source? And why is it that some meditation experiences can be so intense and otherworldly?

I believe that we have been tapping into the same thing: We literally have all the necessary chemicals in the very centre of our brains to create DMT and chemicals that prolong and magnify its effects.[25]

I hope that this helps people who have experienced very intense intuitive or altered states of consciousness to feel more validated in their experiences and to know that there is something just that little stretch further than spiritual philosophy alone to explain these experiences. I also hope that this piques enough interest to warrant further exploration into this possibility because what it could mean for our understanding of depth psychology and intuitive phenomena could be profound.

---

25 Rick Strassman, *DMT: The Spirit Molecule: A Doctor's Revolutionary Research into the Biology of Near-Death and Mystical Experiences* (Park Street Press, 2001).

What Is DMT?

N-Dimethyltryptamine, otherwise known as DMT, is an extremely powerful psychedelic drug first chemically synthesised by Canadian chemist R. Manske.[26] He was intrigued by tryptamine compounds because they occurred in a toxic North American plant called the strawberry shrub; DMT was one of those compounds.[27] It naturally occurs in several plants, including *Mimosa tenuiflora*, *Diplopterys cabrerana*, and *Psychotria viridis*.[28] It can also be found in the secretion of the parotid glands of the *Bufo alvarius* toad.[29]

When consumed recreationally, DMT induces powerful psychedelic effects. Its effects are typically short-lived but incredibly intense. These effects can include:[30,31]

- Intense visual and auditory hallucinations like vivid colours, geometric patterns, and otherworldly entities
- Altered sense of time and reality
- Profound emotional experiences
- Significant realisations

---

26 Tom John Wolff, "Research About DMT and Ayahuasca," in *The Touristic Use of Ayahuasca in Peru: Expectations, Experiences, Meanings and Subjective Effects* (Springer VS Wiesbaden, 2020).

27 Richard H. F. Manske, "A Synthesis of Methyltryptamines and Some Derivatives," *Canadian Journal of Research* 5, no. 5 (1931): 592–600, https://doi.org/10.1139/cjr31-097.

28 Enno Freye, "Dimethyltryptamine (DMT) a Psychedelic," in *Pharmacology and Abuse of Cocaine, Amphetamines, Ecstasy and Related Designer Drugs* (Springer, 2009).

29 Barbara E. Bauer, "5-MeO-DMT, Toad Secretions, and the Entourage Effect," *Psychedelic Science Review*, May 16, 2019, https://psychedelicreview.com/5-meo-dmt-toad-venom-and-the-entourage-effect.

30 Rick Strassman, *DMT: The Spirit Molecule: A Doctor's Revolutionary Research into the Biology of Near-Death and Mystical Experiences* (Park Street Press, 2001).

31 David E. Nichols, "Psychedelics," *Pharmacological Reviews* 68, no. 2 (2016): 264–355, https://doi.org/10.1124/pr.115.011478.

These trips have been described as "breaking through" to a different realm or dimension of consciousness. Many users report vivid hallucinations and altered perceptions of time and space.[32]

DMT is most known for the mystery of its presence in the human body, particularly for the popular theory that it is released in the body both at birth and in death, when consciousness enters and leaves the body.[33]

Deep Experiences in Meditation vs. the Psychedelic Experience

You might be asking yourself, what on earth could DMT or psychedelics possibly have to do with intuition or inner knowing? Why am I bringing it up?

When taken recreationally, psychedelics can take people into a deeply altered state of consciousness. They are known to become completely immersed in a deep and vivid experience of their unconscious as the barrier between their conscious mind and unconscious becomes loosened.[34]

As we have explored before, the subconscious mind is where intuitive insights come from and where one may experience the collective unconscious, which is a shared reservoir of archetypal knowledge, the place in the mind that Jung believed was the source of the information reported by clairvoyants.

---

32 Rick Strassman, *DMT: The Spirit Molecule: A Doctor's Revolutionary Research into the Biology of Near-Death and Mystical Experiences* (Park Street Press, 2001).

33 Rick Strassman, *DMT: The Spirit Molecule: A Doctor's Revolutionary Research into the Biology of Near-Death and Mystical Experiences* (Park Street Press, 2001).

34 Robin L. Carhart-Harris and K. J. Friston, "REBUS and the Anarchic Brain: Toward a Unified Model of the Brain Action of Psychedelics," *Pharmacological Reviews* 71, no. 3 (2019): 316–344, https://doi.org/10.1124/pr.118.017160.

The Shared Phenomena of Religious or Spiritual Experiences in Meditations and Psychedelic Experiences

Many people have experienced profound breakthroughs or insight during psychedelic experiences, which we will explore further later in this chapter. Many people have also claimed to have had deeply "religious" experiences in both meditations and psychedelic experiences.

Psychedelic Experiences

When people take psychedelic trips, it's not uncommon for them to hallucinate religious symbols or even characters appearing to give them some significant form of spoken insight.[35] Another common experience that people have when dealing with particularly strong psychedelic doses is seeing geometry patterns everywhere, with fractal geometry forms showing up as a recurring theme.[36]

Meditation and Ancient Philosophy Links

Meditation is often used to try and connect to different gods or symbols of divine guidance, and as we have explored, there is an actual psychology for the depth of wisdom and intuitive insight that you are

---

35   Rick Strassman, *DMT: The Spirit Molecule: A Doctor's Revolutionary Research into the Biology of Near-Death and Mystical Experiences* (Park Street Press, 2001).

36   A. D. J. Makin et al., "Symmetry Perception and Psychedelic Experience," *Symmetry* 15, no. 7 (2023): 1340, https://doi.org/10.3390/sym15071340.

able to encounter in states of meditation. In shamanic meditations, you are encouraged to establish contact with a "spirit guide" to ask for guidance.

As in psychedelic experiences, experienced meditation practitioners have been known to perceive geometry in deep states of meditation.[37] Many people also believe that if you meditate on certain geometric shapes, like yantras and other sacred geometry shapes, you connect to different forms of meditation.

Thousands of years ago, people in very deep states of meditation were tapping into the same archetypal symbols from the depths of the collective unconscious as those seen in the psychedelic experience. Both meditators and those on psychedelic journeys may experience the unconscious mind in its depths.

I believe that either a subjective sensitivity to the DMT compound in the body, the presence of this compound in different concentrations, or a directed awareness of endogenous DMT in the body can somehow enable this kind of experience.

DMT in the Body

To properly understand this compound's role in the body, let's dig a little into the actual biology. We know for sure that DMT has been found in our bodies and in our brains. It is speculated that it is produced in our pineal gland in particular, a.k.a. the third eye!

The fact that it could be produced in the pineal gland was so significant to me, knowing that the pineal gland has been called "the house of consciousness" and seen as a centre for creativity and

---

[37] Keaki Bryant, "Unveiling the Mystery of Meditation's Geometric Visions," ShunSpirit, September 27, 2024, https://shunspirit.com/article/why-do-i-see-geometric-shapes-when-i-meditate.

intuition in spirituality, while psychedelics have also been used in spiritual practice with the belief that their use enhances your creativity and intuition.

For a period of time, I was really into chakra meditations. When there was something that I wanted to know, I would focus on the centre of my forehead to find answers, which is the third eye chakra centre in Hindu and Buddhist beliefs.

Once I got into a nice deep state of meditation, I would focus my awareness on the centre of my forehead until my awareness of everything else around me completely dissolved. I would then ask myself questions for which I wanted answers or inner guidance before being able to reach substantial inner sources of information.

How to Do a Simple Third Eye Meditation

1. Start by finding a comfortable place where you know you aren't going to be interrupted, making sure that your phone is on silent. Sit with your spine straight, either with your legs crossed or on a chair with your feet grounded on the floor. Rest your hands on your knees or lap with your palms facing upwards. Gently close your eyes.

2. Take in a slow deep breath through your nose, hold it at the top, and then exhale slowly through your mouth. Repeat for five to ten breaths until your mind settles.

3. Bring your attention to the centre of your forehead. Ground your awareness here and imagine an indigo light growing brighter and warmer with every breath you take in. With every exhalation, imagine any mental noise dissolving into the light.

4. After a few moments, imagine the indigo light expanding, gently connecting you to clarity and peace. If you feel any sensations, simply observe without judgment.

5. In this space, ask yourself the question on which you would like insight before letting go of any pressure as far as the outcome and allowing yourself to see whatever emerges. It could come in the form of a feeling, images that pop into your head, or linear insights. The more space and attention you give to the initial feeling that arises, the more that you will be able to see clarity in it.

   Here are some of the best kinds of questions I have found to ask yourself in meditations:

   - How is this situation likely to end up if I choose this path as opposed to another path?
   - Why do I get a bad feeling about this person?
   - What is holding me back from what I hope to accomplish?
   - Have I outgrown my old desires?
   - What new vision would feel most in alignment with me?
   - What opportunities have I been blind to?

6. Take a deep breath in, inhaling fully, and slowly open your eyes. Take a moment to note how you feel.

Pro Tip: This is the perfect meditation to do before journaling.

Could this be an ancient way of tapping into the DMT in the brain or somehow stimulating pineal gland activity that produces DMT? Could simple awareness really be enough to make a difference substantial enough to have such an effect on your psychology or neurobiology?

It seems that Buddhism and Hinduism seem to assume something quite similar.

DMT in the Brain

DMT was first found in the brains and pineal glands of mice and rats, which uncovered the pathways by which animal bodies make this powerful psychedelic.[38]

It was not long before scientists discovered human biochemical pathways similar to those in animals, pathways by which the human body made DMT.[39] DMT became the first endogenous human psychedelic.[40] (Endogenous means a compound made in the body.) Scientists also discovered DMT forming enzymes in samples of lung tissue.[41]

Julius Axelrod, a Nobel prize winning scientist who conducted research from the mid-1900s through 2004, reported finding DMT in human brain tissue.[42] Additional research showed that DMT could also be found in human urine and in the cerebrospinal fluid bathing the brain, which is significant because the pineal gland produces

---

[38] Rick Strassman, *DMT: The Spirit Molecule: A Doctor's Revolutionary Research into the Biology of Near-Death and Mystical Experiences* (Park Street Press, 2001).

[39] Rick Strassman, *DMT: The Spirit Molecule: A Doctor's Revolutionary Research into the Biology of Near-Death and Mystical Experiences* (Park Street Press, 2001).

[40] Steven A. Barker, "N, N-Dimethyltryptamine (DMT), an Endogenous Hallucinogen: Past, Present, and Future Research to Determine Its Role and Function," *Frontiers in Neuroscience* 12 (2018), https://doi.org/10.3389/fnins.2018.00536.

[41] J. G. Dean et al., "Biosynthesis and Extracellular Concentrations of N,N-dimethyltryptamine (DMT) in Mammalian Brain," *Scientific Reports* 9 (2019), https://doi.org/10.1038/s41598-019-45812-w.

[42] David Luke, "Discarnate Entities and Dimethyltryptamine (DMT): Psychopharmacology, Phenomenology and Ontology," *Journal of the Society for Psychical Research* 75, no. 902 (2011): 26–42, https://docslib.org/doc/4959812/discarnate-entities-and-dimethyltryptamine-dmt-psychopharmacology-phenomenology-and-ontology.

melatonin.[43,44] Melatonin is primarily released into the cerebrospinal fluid.[45] Melatonin has an extremely similar chemical structure to DMT, which strengthens the link between DMT and the pineal gland/third eye.[46]

Focusing on bringing the cerebrospinal fluid up your spine is also what is now understood to be a method that has been used to stimulate the "third eye" in an ancient practice related to what is called kundalini.

Kundalini Meditation

The traditional method in yogic traditions called kundalini meditation is an ancient practice focused on awakening a dormant spiritual energy symbolised as a serpent coiled at the base of the spine. The aim is to guide this energy upward through the spine and the body's energy centres, or chakras, culminating at the third eye (or pineal gland). This practice has long been considered a way to expand awareness, intuitive perception, and mystical experiences.

Inspired by these ancient principles, Dr. Joe Dispenza explored his own scientific interpretation of the principles behind kundalini and developed a modern technique known as the "Breath of the Pineal."

---

43 Steven A. Barker, Ethan H. McIlhenny, and Rick Strassman, "A Critical Review of Reports of Endogenous Psychedelic N, N dimethyltryptamines in Humans: 1955–2010," *Drug Testing and Analysis* 4, no. 7–8 (2012): 617–635, https://doi.org/10.1002/dta.422.

44 "Melatonin: What You Need to Know," National Center for Complementary and Integrative Health, last modified May 2024, https://www.nccih.nih.gov/health/melatonin-what-you-need-to-know.

45 Russel J. Reiter et al., "Melatonin in Ventricular and Subarachnoid Cerebrospinal Fluid: Its Function in the Neural Glymphatic Network and Biological Significance for Neurocognitive Health," *Biochemical and Biophysical Research Communications* 605 (2022): 70–81, https://doi.org/10.1016/j.bbrc.2022.03.025.

46 J. G. Dean, "Indolethylamine-N-methyltransferase Polymorphisms: Genetic and Biochemical Approaches for Study of Endogenous N,N,-dimethyltryptamine," *Frontiers in Neuroscience* 12 (2018), https://doi.org/10.3389/fnins.2018.00232.

His method combines breathwork and focused visualisation to activate the pineal gland.

In this meditation, practitioners squeeze the perineum and visualise cerebrospinal fluid being drawn up the spine toward the brain, as if sucking fluid through a straw. This action is believed to put mechanical pressure on the pineal gland.

In this meditation, you may feel slight dizziness, tingling sensations, or a state of euphoria, but such effects are completely normal.[47] If you have a medical condition such as high blood pressure, I recommend consulting a doctor before trying this method.

How to Do Joe Dispenza's Interpretation: Pineal Gland Activating Meditation

1. Make sure that you are somewhere you can fully let go and relax, in a place where you won't be interrupted by anyone around you, and check that your phone notifications are turned off.

2. Sit upright either on a chair or with your legs crossed. Make sure that your spine and neck are straight before placing your hands on your knees.

3. Begin by bringing your awareness to your breath and taking big, slow, deep breaths.

4. As you inhale, contract your muscles in a sequence. First squeeze your perineum (your root area, as in Kegel exercises), then the lower abdomen, and finally the upper abdomen. This creates a pumping action to push energy and cerebrospinal fluid up the

---

[47] Richard W. Maxwell and Sucharit Katyal, "Characteristics of Kundalini-Related Sensory, Motor, and Affective Experiences During Tantric Yoga Meditation," *Frontiers in Psychology* 13 (2022), https://doi.org/10.3389/fpsyg.2022.863091.

spine toward the brain. Clench for a few seconds and then relax your muscles as you exhale slowly through your mouth.

5. Try to direct your awareness up your spine and to your pineal gland in the centre of your head as you inhale, visualising the energy accumulating at the centre of your head.

6. After you have repeated this breath pattern for a few cycles, take one particularly big breath in and squeeze those muscles again, but this time, hold your breath. Aim for 10–30 seconds, or until you feel strain.

7. Exhale slowly through your mouth or nose, relaxing your muscles and allowing yourself to fully unwind.

8. Repeat this breath seven to ten times or more depending on your practice level. A full session is likely to take between ten and fifteen minutes.

9. Before you are ready to close the session, allow yourself some time to fully relax and notice the sensations you feel in your body and how you feel in your emotional state before wiggling your fingers and toes, bringing your awareness into the room, and opening your eyes.

Rick Strassman

Rick Strassman, the first US scientist funded to conduct psychedelic research since the War on Drugs in the '70s, explored the purpose of DMT in the brain and the high probability that it is produced in the pineal gland, and he came to some fascinating conclusions. He figured out that the unique enzymes which convert serotonin, melatonin, or tryptamine into psychedelic compounds are present in extraordinarily high concentrations in the pineal gland, which is what is needed to make DMT and DMT effect prolonging chemicals.[48]

Through his research, Strassman started to come to spiritual conclusions; he began to regard the pineal gland as the spirit gland and DMT as the spirit molecule. He performed a series of tests and trials to understand DMT, its effects on the mind, and the nature of experiences such as astral projection and near-death experiences, suspecting that they could be linked.

Strassman hypothesised that our body gets a big flood of DMT during both birth and death. He observed that the pineal gland could be the most active part of the body in death and came to the conclusion that the life force exists in the body is the pineal gland.[49] The body gets a big chemical surge in death, and many people who have had a near-death experience describe it as deeply psychedelic and profound in nature.[50]

People who have experienced NDEs (near-death experiences) often experience:[51]

- Feeling detached from the body, often observing it from above
- Vivid visuals and sensations that may include bright lights, tunnels, geometric patterns, or encounters with entities
- An altered perception of time
- Profound emotional impact

---

48 Rick Strassman, *DMT: The Spirit Molecule: A Doctor's Revolutionary Research into the Biology of Near-Death and Mystical Experiences* (Park Street Press, 2001).

49 Rick Strassman, *DMT: The Spirit Molecule: A Doctor's Revolutionary Research into the Biology of Near-Death and Mystical Experiences* (Park Street Press, 2001).

50 Mary M. Sweeney et al., "Comparison of Psychedelic and Near-Death or Other Non-Ordinary Experiences in Changing Attitudes About Death and Dying," *PLOS One* 17, no. 8 (2022): e0271926, https://doi.org/10.1371/journal.pone.0271926.

51 "Near-Death Experiences," *Psychology Today*, https://www.psychologytoday.com/us/basics/near-death-experiences?msockid=399532b88aff6a7d3c1c242a8bf36b11.

Near-Death Experience in Surgery

Pam Reynolds underwent brain surgery in 1991 for a life-threatening aneurysm. During the procedure, her body cooled, and her heart stopped. She reported an out-of-body experience, and she described observing the surgical team from above, accurately describing tools and conversations despite being under anaesthesia. She also described moving through a tunnel toward a bright light and encountering deceased relatives who provided comfort. Her account is one of the most well-documented near-death experiences, with many details later verified by the medical staff involved in her procedure.[52]

It's hypothesized that DMT is released when we are in high stress, which could explain why this kind of phenomenon is so common in near-death experiences.[53]

Links Between Trauma, Intuition, and Pineal Gland Function

"The wound is where the light enters you."
— Rumi[54]

I used to work in a small metaphysical gift shop doing intuitive readings in a room downstairs, seated in front of a prop crystal ball. One of the

---

52   "Pam Reynolds Near Death Experience," The NDE, https://www.neardth.com/pam-reynolds-nde.php.

53   Dionysios Grammenos and Steven A. Barker, "On the Transmethylation Hypothesis: Stress, N,N-dimethyltryptamine, and Positive Symptoms of Psychosis," *Journal of Neural Transmission* 122 (2015): 733–739, https://doi.org/10.1007/s00702-014-1329-5.

54   Reynold A. Nicholson, *The Mathnawí of Jalálu'ddín Rúmí* (Messrs. Luzac & Co., 1926).

women who worked there told me two stories on the topic of intuition that have stayed with me.

The first was from her experience of childbirth. She vividly remembered a sweet older woman with large glasses sitting by her side comforting her through the pain. But after asking the nurses who the woman was, she learned there had been no such person present. Her description, however, matched a patient who had recently passed away nearby.

The second story was about a man she knew, an amputee who had suffered a traumatic accident and a near-death experience. After his recovery, he found himself unusually intuitive. He could sense things about people that logic couldn't explain.

What do these cases have in common? Stress.

Over time I noticed a pattern. Often the most intuitive people I met were also the most creative, and nearly all had been through some kind of significant trauma or ego death. It was almost as if these experiences seemed to crack something open in them.

If DMT and the pineal gland were somehow involved in intuitive and creative states, could extreme stress or trauma trigger a shift in the brain that aligns with these awakenings or psychological shifts?

Rick Strassman speculated that stress might stimulate the production of endogenous DMT. He even suggested that "runner's high" might be linked to production of very low levels of DMT. In his studies with small doses of DMT, patients described sensations identical to runner's high: "A shimmering and brightening of the visual field; a sense of lightness, as if floating; and a profound slowing of time."[55]

In 2013, Dr. Jimo Borjigin and her team at the University of Michigan studied rats during cardiac arrest. They observed a sudden

---

55   Rick Strassman, *DMT: The Spirit Molecule: A Doctor's Revolutionary Research into the Biology of Near-Death and Mystical Experiences* (Park Street Press, 2001).

surge in high-frequency gamma brain waves; patterns typically associated with heightened conscious awareness. These brain states were more active than those during normal waking life. Although the study didn't directly measure DMT, it suggested the brain may enter a heightened state of consciousness under extreme stress, possibly opening the door to profound experiences.[56]

Birth and death, during which it is hypothesised that DMT is released in the body, are extremely stressful times. Floods of stress-related hormones are released at these times, including the pineal gland stimulating catecholamines, adrenaline, and noradrenaline.[57,58,59]

Strassman observed that the birth experience is highly psychedelic for an unanaesthetised mother who undergoes extreme pain and stress, and he also stated it's likely that it's pretty psychedelic for the newborn, too.[60] We know that DMT is present in newborn laboratory animals. It could also be present in newborn humans, although no one has yet looked for DMT in human newborns or their mothers during delivery.[61]

---

56 Jimo Borjigin et al., "Surge of Neurophysiological Coherence and Connectivity in the Dying Brain," *Proceedings of the National Academy of Sciences* 110, no. 35 (2013): 14432–14437, https://doi.org/10.1073/pnas.1308285110.

57 Jimo Borjigin et al., "Surge of Neurophysiological Coherence and Connectivity in the Dying Brain," *Proceedings of the National Academy of Sciences* 110, no. 35 (2013): 14432–14437, https://doi.org/10.1073/pnas.1308285110.

58 Brianna Chu et al. *Physiology, Stress Reaction* (StatPearls Publishing, 2025).

59 Pär Ingemar Johansson et al., "High Circulating Adrenaline Levels at Admission Predict Increased Mortality After Trauma," *The Journal of Trauma and Acute Care Surgery* 72, no. 2 (2012): 428–436, https://doi.org/10.1097/ta.0b013e31821e0f93.

60 Rick Strassman, *DMT: The Spirit Molecule: A Doctor's Revolutionary Research into the Biology of Near-Death and Mystical Experiences* (Park Street Press, 2001).

61 J. G. Dean et al., "Biosynthesis and Extracellular Concentrations of N,N-dimethyltryptamine (DMT) in Mammalian Brain," *Scientific Reports* 9 (2019), https://doi.org/10.1038/s41598-019-45812-w.

Normal vaginal delivery produces an enormous outpouring of catecholamine release.[62] The massive flooding of these stress hormones over both the mother's and foetus's pineal glands may be enough to override the pineal defence system and set in motion DMT release, according to Strassman.[63] He said, "The birth experience is highly psychedelic for the unanaesthetised mother—how much more for the child?"[64]

If the mother is anesthetized, catecholamine production is decreased, and if the baby is delivered by caesarean section, even less catecholamine is produced. Therefore, these latter two situations may result in less robust, if any, DMT release by the mother's and baby's pineal glands.[65] To further strengthen this link, you might find interesting that Stanislav Grof, a psychotherapist who researched psychedelic experiences, found that during psychedelic therapy, those who were born by caesarean section were less likely to "let go" than those who were born vaginally.[66]

I felt a need to more directly investigate the implications of enhanced intuitive ability during such experiences and potential links to stress. It turns out that there is a strong and often debated connection

---

62   K. Hägnevik et al., "Catecholamine Surge and Metabolic Adaptation in the Newborn After Vaginal Delivery and Caesarean Section," *Acta Paediatrica* 73, no. 5 (1984): 602–609, https://doi.org/10.1111/j.1651-2227.1984.tb09982.x.

63   Rick Strassman, *DMT: The Spirit Molecule: A Doctor's Revolutionary Research into the Biology of Near-Death and Mystical Experiences* (Park Street Press, 2001).

64   Rick Strassman, *DMT: The Spirit Molecule: A Doctor's Revolutionary Research into the Biology of Near-Death and Mystical Experiences* (Park Street Press, 2001).

65   Rick Strassman, *DMT: The Spirit Molecule: A Doctor's Revolutionary Research into the Biology of Near-Death and Mystical Experiences* (Park Street Press, 2001).

66   Stanislav Grof, *Realms of the Human Unconscious: Observations from LSD Research* (Dutton, 1976).

between trauma and the development of heightened sensitivity or intuition.[67]

Birth and death are the times that consciousness enters and leaves our body. Pain has also been observed as a factor that some believe is necessary for the expansion of consciousness. Alan Watts once asserted, "There is no coming to consciousness without pain."[68]

So, what we already know about the pineal gland and various existing beliefs that it is the house of consciousness becomes fascinating and makes me question if DMT could have anything to do with consciousness in itself.

Psychedelics and the Development of Human Consciousness

Terence McKenna, a famous philosopher and psychonaut, called psychedelics "technologies" and "sacraments" that amplify the mind's ability to perceive deeper structures of reality.[69] He even popularised a hypothesis he called "the stoned ape theory" in which he proposed that psychedelics played a key role in the evolution of human consciousness.

The theory posits that psychedelic mushrooms ingested by prehuman hominids enhanced visual acuity, leading to increased hunting success and social cohesion. He also proposed that the altered states of consciousness induced by the mushrooms contributed to the emergence of language, art, and religious experiences.

---

67   Sarah Dyanne Stanton, "Intuition: A Silver Lining for Clinicians with Complex Trauma" (master's thesis, Syracuse University, 2016), https://surface.syr.edu/etd/615.
68   Alan W. Watts, *The Wisdom of Insecurity: A Message for an Age of Anxiety* (Pantheon Books, 1951).
69   Terence McKenna, *Food of the Gods: The Search for the Original Tree of Knowledge* (Bantam, 1993).

This theory is not supported by mainstream science today due to its speculative claims about evolution and a lack of empirical evidence, and I myself would not agree with it entirely, but I still believe that there is some value in some of the points he made. Perhaps when we as early humans expanded our level of consciousness, it was connected with something of a psychedelic nature; then again, perhaps psychedelics never had to be ingested in the first place, but rather this transformation was something that took place more internally.

The effect that psychedelics have on the brain can be profoundly expansive. These substances have been shown to enhance neuroplasticity, which is the brain's ability to reorganize itself by forming new neural connections, a process which supports adaptability, learning, and openness to new ways of thinking.[70]

This heightened neuroplasticity can be essential for mental and emotional growth. Psychedelics also temporarily disrupt the Default Mode Network (DMN), which is a system in the brain associated with ego and habitual thought patterns. By softening the grip of the DMN, the brain is able to operate in a more flexible, interconnected manner often described as a "reset," and this can help break cycles of rumination and rigid thinking.[71]

Both heightened neuroplasticity and the partial ego dissolution described above are associated with expansion of awareness and

---

70 Steven F. Grieco et al., "Psychedelics and Neural Plasticity: Therapeutic Implications," *The Journal of Neuroscience* 42, no. 45 (2022): 8439–8449, https://doi.org/10.1523/jneurosci.1121-22.2022.

71 Robin L. Carhart-Harris et al., "The Entropic Brain: A Theory of Conscious States Informed by Neuroimaging Research with Psychedelic Drugs," *Frontiers in Human Neuroscience* 8 (2014), https://doi.org/10.3389/fnhum.2014.00020.

therefore of consciousness.[72] Both of these things have been proven to be possible to achieve with a meditation practice.[73]

Many cultures with strong meditation traditions use psychedelics consciously, each in their own ways of ritual and ceremony. However, when it comes to their beliefs about what psychedelics do, there is a great deal of commonality and crossover between many cultures as far as the view that these substances allow one to see through to another realm and may help one to reach some kind of divine insight. Some cultures even use psychedelics with the belief that they enable one to speak to God directly.

Psychedelia in Spiritual and Religious History

Psychedelics have at times been used not as recreational drugs but rather as "medicine" in ritualistic and ceremonial contexts to expand consciousness and gain deeper wisdom and insight.

72   Robin L. Carhart-Harris et al., "The Entropic Brain: A Theory of Conscious States Informed by Neuroimaging Research with Psychedelic Drugs," *Frontiers in Human Neuroscience* 8 (2014), https://doi.org/10.3389/fnhum.2014.00020.

73   Yi-Yuan Tang et al., "The Neuroscience of Mindfulness Meditation," *Nature Reviews Neuroscience* 16 (2015): 213–225, https://doi.org/10.1038/nrn3916.

Native American Traditions: Peyote

Many Native American tribes used peyote as a religious sacrament for thousands of years before Europeans arrived. The ingestion of peyote during all-night prayer ceremonies is a key part of the practices of the Native American Church. Over forty tribes in North America, including western Canada, still use it ceremonially.[74]

Peyote is a small spineless cactus that has hallucinogenic properties; when eaten in a ritual context, it is believed to enable the individual to commune with God and spirits through visions.[75]

Ayahuasca and Psilocybin Mushrooms

Shamans are also known to take psychoactive plants and fungi as spiritual medicines. Ayahuasca and psilocybin mushrooms are commonly used to connect to the spirit realm. There is a great deal of mushroom iconography in indigenous artifacts, such as mushroom stones, which have been speculated to be linked to psychedelic culture.

Ancient Greek "Magic Potion"

In 1978, there was a book published called *The Road to Eleusis: Unveiling the Secret of the Mysteries,* which revealed insights into the mystery rituals of this spiritual capital of the ancient world. For two thousand years, pilgrims would trek to this temple to drink a "magic potion" known as *kykeon* and become divine to face their fear of death.

In an attempt to make sense of how so many people could have consistently experienced revolutionary states during the main

---

74   Omer C. Stewart, *Peyote Religion: A History* (University of Oklahoma Press, 1993).

75   Ruth Shonle, "Peyote, the Giver of Visions," *American Anthropologist* 27, no. 1 (1925): 53–75, https://www.jstor.org/stable/661497.

ceremony of the Eleusinian Mysteries, a hypothesis was developed theorising that the barley used in the Eleusinian kykeon contained ergot, a psychedelic containing LSD-like psychedelic alkaloids. Ergot was discovered in a temple at the Mas Castellar site both inside a vase and within the dental calculus of a twenty-five-year-old man, providing evidence of ergot being consumed and supporting this theory.[76]

Psychedelic References in the Bible

There have even been suspected references to psychedelics in the Bible. Some scholars in Jerusalem believe that the burning bush that Moses spoke to in the Bible was actually the acacia bush, which is rich in DMT. In the biblical story of Moses, the burning bush was God speaking to him.

The King James version of Exodus 16:14 gives a description of manna that seems very similar to mushrooms in shape and location and even the time of day that they appear.

Amazonian Tribes

In the mid-1800s, two European explorers, Richard Spruce from England and Alexander von Humboldt from Germany, found themselves deep in the Amazon, where they encountered something unexpected: powerful mind-altering snuffs and brews crafted from visionary plants by indigenous tribes.

These plant medicines, which were known by many names—including *yopo*, *epená*, and *jurema*—were used ceremonially to open

---

[76] Giorgio Samorini, "The Oldest Archeological Data Evidencing the Relationship of *Homo sapiens* with Psychoactive Plants: A Worldwide Overview," *Journal of Psychedelic Studies* 3, no. 2 (2019): 63–80, https://doi.org/10.1556/2054.2019.008.

portals of perception. They would blow the powdered snuff through a long pipe directly into another person's nostrils with so much force that it could send the receiver straight to the ground due to the sheer intensity of the experience.

Spruce and Humboldt observed these ceremonies from the sidelines; they never took part themselves, but they watched as tribal participants entered deep, altered states, trembling, purging, speaking incoherently.

The locals spoke of visions and astral travel, as well as being able to find missing objects, foresee future events, and even commune with the dead.

Psychedelic Testing and Observations

Author Brian C. Muraresku says it is claimed that during psilocybin experiments, atheists were known to start speaking of God after just one trip and that this reaction was not at all uncommon.[77]

Albert Hoffman, who famously synthesized LSD while in pursuit of finding a migraine medicine, observed that LSD caused a psychic loosening or opening. He used to take LSD in his back garden and claimed he "saw the hand of God there." and had profound experiences which he described as divine.[78]

These experiences seem to open people's minds to deep revelation so strongly experienced that they describe it as divine, or it makes them believe in God or external wiser metaphysical entities. They experience such deep insight that in many cases, it's not even interpreted as a part of themselves. Sure, it's not a part of their conscious thinking minds,

---

[77] Brian C. Muraresku, *The Immortality Key: The Secret History of the Religion with No Name* (St. Martin's Press, 2020).

[78] Albert Hofmann, *LSD: My Problem Child*, trans. Jonathan Ott (McGraw-Hill, 1980).

which might be what creates this divide, but it's within them. This shocking and mystifying level of wisdom is within us all, regardless of what you believe in.

A Psychedelic Experience of Psychic Phenomena

A story that was related to me adds more on the link between psychedelics and intuitive phenomena. I was once speaking to a friend in her kitchen about the role of DMT in the body and how I suspected it had potential links to intuitive experiences. Her brother overheard me and was quick to butt in to tell me about an experience that he and his friend had on LSD.

My friend's brother told me that once when he was with two other friends, he decided to take LSD with one while the other friend stayed sober. He said that during this trip, he was having a conversation with his friend who was also on LSD. After the trip, they spoke about that conversation again; but their sober friend said, "What are you talking about? You were silent the whole time!"

So the two who were on the psychedelic trip did not say a word out loud, yet both of them could remember the conversation that they had word for word. Bear in mind that these were two young men who almost certainly had not been influenced by spiritual philosophies, let alone by any cultural belief that such telepathy was possible.

Mystical Experiences in Meditation

You may have heard stories of people having profound mystical experiences like hearing a guiding voice, imagining angels, out-of-body experiences, or premonitions in meditation.

Astral Projection

After having experienced a profound out-of-body experience in meditation, I remember thinking to myself, "I can't imagine a psychedelic experience is much more intense than that." I believe this is the primary reason why I connected so much to the idea that there was deep significance in the links between mystical and intuitive experiences and DMT.

Ironically, I was meditating with no other intention but to soothe my anxiety. I started out with simple breathwork and just let whatever wanted to surface arise. Then I put my awareness on my breath and breathed very slowly. As I was doing this meditative breathing, about ten minutes in, I started to get this strong sensation in my head that dominated my awareness, particularly as I exhaled. It felt like there was pressure on my head that kept getting stronger. Then it felt like I was rapidly falling backward, and it also felt a little tingly, and then I felt these sensations in my entire body.

Something snapped: There was a flash of light, a bang, this vast feeling of expansion, and then I was suspended in this dark black space.

I specifically remember trying to find my breath and realising that I couldn't find it if I tried, which I had never experienced before. There was no inhale or exhale, and I couldn't feel my body. I remember thinking seriously, "Have I died halfway through my meditation?"

Things got stranger; I remember simultaneously hearing and feeling a growing sensation of vibration that arose as I saw these multicoloured droplets simultaneously squirming around each other and multiplying. After a time, they were everywhere; the vibration sensation was loud, and I was being shaken so vigorously that my vision began to blur; and I felt that pressure again, I could really feel it. It was a strong sensation.

Then I was back in my body, in my own room. It was not a dreamlike feeling; it was nothing like anything that I could have imagined. It was a very real feeling, and while it was going on, I didn't feel in control of the experience.

This experience shifted my perspective.

This meditation changed how I viewed the world and how I thought about the way we experience things individually. It was an experience I had while I was sober, and it was so strange, so different. I could have easily gone my whole life without knowing that such a feeling even existed. I might have even passively dismissed anyone who might have claimed it was possible.

I remember later speaking about it with someone who had experimented with DMT; he told me that what I had experienced sounded exactly like a DMT experience—short-lived, vivid, and featuring out-of-body experience, colours, sensations, and sounds, right down to the vibration. This is definitely the most intense thing that I have ever experienced, I can say that with absolute confidence.

I was a broken record speaking about it to my friends as I tried to wrap my head around it and process this alien experience. I even remember feeling a bit cursed—I'd had this intense profound experience, but I could never communicate it without sounding like a madman because I had never known anyone to experience anything remotely like this in a sober state.

Although to some it is a question of whether what I experienced is even possible, some people dedicate a lot of their time to being able to achieve such states in meditation and meditate specifically for these out-of-body experiences. After this experience, I became very interested in this practice and did a lot of research on astral projection.

If you ever wanted to try to have an experience such as this, here is what I have learned about astral projection as a conscious act.

Astral Projection Guide

It's important to note that this is quite an advanced practice. If you have never meditated before, this will be a tricky practice to get into right away. The ability to direct your awareness and enter different states of consciousness as an act of will is crucial for this practice. Astral projection is not likely to happen the first time you practice this kind of meditation, but the more you practice it, the more you will be able to connect with it and the higher your chances of experiencing astral projection.

Pro Tips:

- Make sure that you have not eaten anything too heavy in the past two hours. Astral projection—or any kind of meditation that requires visionary ability—is best done on a light stomach.

- This practice is best done in the evening but not too close to the hour when you usually go to bed since you need to be relaxed but not sleepy.

- When lying down for this practice, don't lie down on your bed as you are more likely to fall asleep if you do.

- During the practice, try not to feel fear; it's a natural blocker.

THE MEDITATION

1. Start by making sure that you are in a quiet and comfortable space where you won't be disturbed: Ensure that your phone is on silent, wear loose clothing, and dim the lights or use soft lighting like candles.

2. Lie down flat on your back and gently close your eyes. Take slow, deep breaths. Inhale deeply through your nose, hold for a few seconds, and deeply exhale through your mouth. Gradually relax each part of your body by bringing your awareness into each body part one at a time, starting from your toes and moving up to your head.

3. Next you want to achieve a hypnagogic or deep meditative state, which is a state between wakefulness and sleep. Keep your attention awake while you allow the rest of your mind to gradually drift off into sleep. Quietly focus on your breathing, dissolving any thoughts that arise into your exhaled breaths if they arise.

4. Now imagine a second body (your astral body) rising or floating above your physical body. Some people like to visualise a rope hanging above them and pulling themselves up by it. Others prefer imagining gently floating upward.

5. If you feel vibrations or buzzing or hear strange sounds (which are common in the process of astral projection), stay calm. If your emotions shift too dramatically, your awareness will shift back to your body.

6. Once you feel separated from your body, look around and explore. You may be able to move freely or visit distant places.

7. When you are ready to return, simply focus on your intention to re-enter your physical body. You may feel a snap, a slight shock, or a gentle pull.

8. Bring your awareness back to your physical body, wiggle your fingers and toes, and open your eyes.

Here is another meditation you can do to improve your chances of astral projection; this one is good for beginners.

Yoga Nidra

Yoga nidra is a meditation that encourages body awareness. This is a fantastic meditation to start with if you are looking to improve your chances of being able to astral project, and it also has amazing benefits for your health. You will be able to feel more subtle shifts in your body and notice things like catching the flu or other body changes sooner.

THE MEDITATION

1. Begin by preparing a peaceful space where you can fully relax without interruptions. Turn off or silence your phone, and wear soft, loose clothing.

2. Lie comfortably on your back, with your arms resting softly alongside your body, palms facing upward or inward (whichever feels more natural). Close your eyes and take a slow, deep breath in through your nose, then exhale softly through your mouth. Let each breath help you settle more deeply into the surface beneath you.

3. Shift your attention inward, noticing the points where your body makes contact with the floor or bed. Feel the weight of your body grounding you, fully supported by the surface on which it rests.

4. Now, bring gentle awareness to your breath without trying to change it. Observe the natural flow of your inhalations

and exhalations, feeling the subtle rise and fall of your abdomen or chest.

5. Begin a mental journey through your body, and as you focus on each area, invite a sense of warmth and ease to expand there. Start with your feet: Feel warmth spreading through your toes, the soles of your feet, and your ankles. Slowly move upward to your calves, knees, and thighs. Let your legs become heavy and relaxed.

6. Continue to your hips and pelvis. Soften any tightness or tension you notice. Move to your lower back and abdomen, releasing any holding or discomfort.

7. Shift attention to your chest and upper back, breathing gently into these areas, allowing your breath to soften your heart space.

8. Bring awareness to your shoulders, arms, and hands. Feel them relax and melt into the surface beneath you.

9. Finally, bring your focus to your neck, jaw, face, and scalp. Release any tightness, letting your jaw part slightly, your forehead smooth out, and your entire head soften.

10. Remain in this peaceful state, simply resting in the awareness of your body and breath. If your mind wanders, gently bring it back to the sensation of your breath or the warmth of your body.

11. When you feel ready to conclude your practice, slowly deepen your breath and begin to bring movement back to your fingers and toes. Stretch your arms and legs gently if you like. When you feel ready, open your eyes.

Chapter 5

Dream States and the Mystery of 3:00 to 5:00 a.m.

"The dream is a little hidden door in the innermost and most secret recesses of the soul, opening into that cosmic night which was psyche long before there was any ego-consciousness."[79]

—C. G. Jung, "The Meaning of Psychology for Modern Man"

The Magic of Dreams

Perhaps not everyone meditates to explore the wisdom of the depths of their psyche, but there is one thing that we all do: We sleep. Dreams are amazing things for us to learn how to work with, not only

---

[79] Carl G. Jung, "The Meaning of Psychology for Modern Man," in *The Quotable Jung*, ed. Judith R. Harris (Princeton University Press, 2016).

to uncover deeper, more intuitive messages but to help us to gain a deeper understanding of ourselves and clarity on our deeper desires, our fears, and our emotions in general. The experiences we encounter while in deep meditation and engaging the active imagination are very similar to dream states. There are also some interesting connections between the hours when we are most likely to sleep and the pineal gland (or third eye), and these are linked with intuitive traditions and spiritual schools of thought and beliefs.

When Is the Pineal Gland Most Active?

The pineal gland often plays a key role in regulating our sleep/wake cycle by secreting melatonin, which helps the body fall asleep.[80] Melatonin levels usually begin to rise in the evening as light decreases, and these levels generally peak in the body between 2:00 and 4:00 a.m., tapering off as sunrise approaches. This rhythm is deeply influenced by light exposure.[81]

So, the pineal gland is most active around this time, secreting melatonin, which as already discussed has an incredibly similar chemical structure to DMT.

What if DMT is also released within this time frame? Dr. Rick Strassman suspects that DMT, as well as melatonin, is highly influential to dream states. Strassman actually first started to study melatonin in the '80s, at which time there was data suggesting it had psychoactive effects.[82]

---

80   Josephine Arendt and Anna Aulinas, "Physiology of the Pineal Gland and Melatonin," in *Endotext*, ed. K. R. Feingold, S. F. Ahmed, B. Anawalt, et al. (MDText.com, Inc., 2000–), updated October 30, 2022, https://www.ncbi.nlm.nih.gov/books/NBK550972.

81   Theodoros B. Grivas and Olga D. Savvidou, "Melatonin the 'Light of Night' in Human Biology and Adolescent Idiopathic Scoliosis," *Scoliosis* 2 (2007), https://doi.org/10.1186/1748-7161-2-6.

82   Rick J. Strassman et al., "A Model for the Study of the Acute Effects of Melatonin in Man," *Journal of Clinical Endocrinology & Metabolism* 65, no. 5 (1987): 847–852, https://doi.org/10.1210/jcem-65-5-847.

The effects of melatonin only seemed to be sedative, which is why he began to focus more on the properties of DMT to better understand dream states, which can be quite psychedelic in nature.[83]

The most vivid dreams tend to occur between 3:00 and 5:00 a.m., depending on when you fall asleep. During this window, your brain is cycling through its longest and deepest periods of REM (Rapid Eye Movement) sleep.[84]

What if dreams are caused by DMT? They are, after all, mild hallucinations that bring unconscious material to the surface.

The nature of dream states is very similar to DMT trips in the sense of what happens when you come out of the dream or trip. Have you ever had a vivid and complex dream that you felt had so much meaning, yet within a few moments of waking up and getting ready for your morning routine, it's completely gone? All that's left of your experience is the feeling that it left you with. Despite how vivid your experience might have been, you can easily forget if you don't immediately write it down after the experience is over. Strassman made these same observations when he was testing the psychoactive effects of DMT and, as explored before, traces of DMT have been found in both the pineal gland and the cerebrospinal fluid which melatonin is produced in and released into.[85] This is all very speculative, of course, but there are still some strong and fascinating parallels that make it worth questioning.

---

[83] Rick Strassman, *DMT: The Spirit Molecule: A Doctor's Revolutionary Research into the Biology of Near-Death and Mystical Experiences* (Park Street Press, 2001).

[84] Mary A. Carskadon and William C. Dement, "Normal Human Sleep: An Overview," in *Principles and Practice of Sleep Medicine*, 5th ed. (Saunders, 2011).

[85] Sam Woolfe, "How to Integrate a Difficult-to-Remember DMT Experience," Maps of the Mind, March 9, 2020, https://mapsofthemind.com/2020/09/03/how-to-integrate-difficult-remember-dmt-experience/#:~:text=One%20of%20the%20most%20common%20features%20%28and%20frustrations%29,trip%20as%20you%20return%20to%20normal%20waking%20consciousness.

Psychic and Mystical Experiences in Dreams

The most common context in which people experience psychic phenomena is through dream states. You may even be among the third of people who have experienced at least one precognitive or premonition dream.[86] These are dreams that seemingly predict the future.

I myself, along with various other members of my family, have experienced particularly strange dreams that can't be explained—dreams that have come true. My dad and I once even shared an interrelated dream on the same night.

My Dream Phenomena Experiences

Fire Alarm

When I was younger, I had a dream that my school was burning down. The next day at school, I remember being apprehensive and on edge because I had a deep gut feeling about this dream. I even told my friends about it in the morning. When I was sitting in class later during the third or fourth period, the fire bell went off. Someone had set fire to something in food tech, and we all had to evacuate.

---

[86] Helen Marlo, "Precognitive Dreams: When Your Dreams Come True," *Psychology Today*, March 25, 2025, https://www.psychologytoday.com/gb/blog/deeper-dive/202503/precognitive-dreams-when-your-dreams-come-true?msockid=399532b88aff6a7d3c1c242a8bf36b11.

Tsunami

I remember waking up in a friend's house after having had a particularly vivid and disturbing dream that I was at a funeral. There were two graves; in one was my younger brother, but I couldn't see who was in the other one. My dad rang me up later on in the day to say that he'd had a disturbing dream that both he and my brother were caught up in a tsunami. In his dream, the wave crashed over them both before he woke up. So, he had the front end of the story and I had the back end, all in the same night. I am glad to be able to confirm that there was no tsunami and that my dad and brother are both alive and well. I was shocked by the interlinked and vivid nature of our dreams.

On a different day, I remember hearing a voice in my dream in a way similar to what comes across in some of my meditations sometimes, a very wise voice that didn't seem to come from my conscious mind that helped me to solve an issue that I had been stuck on and profoundly changed the way that I viewed things.

Stories of Dream Phenomena in My Family

Strangely intuitive dreams seem to have been quite common on my mum's side of the family. I remember meeting some distant relatives from Poland; one of my mum's cousins told me she had such frequent and intense premonition dreams that it would freak out her co-workers.

My aunt also experienced premonition dreams, and she concluded that déjà vu comes from dreams like these.

Other Dream Phenomena

Even if we are not strictly talking about psychic phenomena or intuitive dreams, dreams can be incredibly trippy and mystical. If you have ever experienced a lucid dream or sleep paralysis, you understand just how strange these experiences can be.

I have had many experiences like these. I have even had a few strange dream experiences in which I was absolutely convinced that I had left my body. These experiences always followed a period of sleep paralysis, which is when your body is still asleep but your mind is very awake and conscious. I was later told by the shaman I was working with at the time that sleep paralysis is sometimes a stage that you have to pass through in order to have an out-of-body experience.

My Astral Projection Experience in Sleep

I remember one particular time when I was a teen; I was looking at my body and trying to make my way downstairs in this new strange form to wake my parents up so that they could wake me up, because I had this awful drowsy feeling in my "astral body." The closer that I got to my bedroom door, the more I felt this magnetic sensation pulling me back to my physical body, and there was this pain in my head that became stronger and stronger the further away I got from my physical body.

Finally, I was pulled back to my physical body, and I woke up. I remember that after I had awoken, the pain in my head returned the more I drifted back into sleep, so then I turned on my bedside light to properly wake up.

Later, when I was in a sixth form philosophy class and the topic of dreams was brought up, my teacher said that it was impossible to feel real pain in dreams, an assertion to which I strongly objected.

The fact that these kinds of strange experiences are more common in dream states makes a lot of sense; these states are the deepest into the subconscious that most people ever come into awareness of without a meditation practice.

Some people say God speaks to them in dreams, or that there is a deeply spiritual significance to dream states, in the same way that meditations or psychedelic experiences are often interpreted.

There are many spiritual, religious, and cultural interpretations around the period of time when we most commonly dream—the hours when the pineal gland is most active. Some say it's a divine or supernatural time, but there has also been superstition focused on this period of time throughout history.

The Significance of 3:00 to 5:00 a.m. in Religion and Cultural Superstitions

The Witching Hour

In folklore, 3:00 to 5:00 a.m. is known as the witching hour or the devil's hour. This is a time of the night that is most associated with supernatural events. The concept of the witching hour can be traced back to ancient times when it was believed that certain hours of the day and night were more auspicious for magic and divination practices. The witching hour in particular was seen as a time when witches and other practitioners of the occult were at their most powerful. In the Middle Ages, people were advised to stay indoors around this time for this reason.

Hinduism

Something about these superstitions that particularly intrigues me is their alignment with the Hindu belief in Brahma Muhurta, which is a time that holds great significance in Hinduism. Brahma Muhurta translates to "time of the Creator"; the time varies, but the bottom line is that it's around one hour and thirty-six minutes before sunrise, typically landing it approximately between 3:30 and 5:00 a.m. It is believed that Brahma Muhurta is the time which is best for meditation and spiritual work because there is a source of immense energy available at that hour which provides the most benefit.

Sadhguru on Brahma Muhurta:

"If you become in rhythm with life, you will wake up somewhere after 3:00 a.m. At this time, you should sit up and do whatever you feel initiated to do [and] it will bear maximum fruit, the seed will get the support that it needs to sprout around this time."[87]

Islam

In Islam, there is an optional night prayer that falls between 3:00 and 5:00 a.m. called *Tahajjud*. It is said that God is more present around these hours and the veils between the realms are at their thinnest.

In Psychology

The hour between 3:00 and 4:00 a.m. has been the subject of much speculation from a psychological standpoint. Some experts believe that it represents a time of transition, a time when the mind is more open

---

[87] Sadhguru, host, *Sadhguru's Podcast*, podcast transcription, "Something Phenomenal Happens at 3:40 AM: Brahma Muhurtam," https://podcasts.happyscribe.com/sadhguru-s-podcast/something-phenomenal-happens-at-3-40-am-sadhguru-brahma-muhurtam.

to ideas and experiences. Others see it as a time of heightened creativity and intuition, when the subconscious mind is more active and receptive to inspiration, all of which are aspects of consciousness that align to the psychology of the mind either on a low dose of psychedelics or during deep meditation.

The similarities are uncanny:

- Enhanced emotional sensitivity
- Enhanced creativity
- Enhanced intuition
- Mind more open to ideas

You can learn how to utilise both your dreams and this creative window for great work in the same way that many renowned creative thinkers in history have used these hours. Many famous creatives have spoken about this time as fertile ground for inspiration.

Creatives Who Utilised This Window

- **Nikola Tesla** reportedly worked and thought best during odd nocturnal hours.
- **Salvador Dali** used to nap with a key in his hand, allowing him to wake up in that semi-dream state when the key dropped and capture surreal images directly from his subconscious.
- **Carl Jung** emphasized the symbolic richness of dream and early-morning material in uncovering the unconscious.

There have been times where I have felt stuck on something in my life, and when I have turned on the lights at 3:00 a.m., it's been then that the answers have come to me. I like the idea that meditation during these hours leads to greater breakthroughs. It makes sense to me that you are able to reach deeper insight in meditation within these hours, especially with what we now understand from the biology and psychology side of things. Again, this shows that the wisdom of these ancient schools of thought can only be a testament to the extent to which the intuitive mind can find truth.

This kind of intuitive and creative psychological phenomena is something that does not affect all people in sleep. What if you are blind and have no perception of sunlight, the thing that feeds back to your pineal gland and sets your circadian rhythms? The answer to this could give us insight into the intuitive archetype of the wise blind man.

Blindsight Phenomena

In reflecting upon circadian rhythms and pineal gland activity, I began to reflect on what kind of possibilities this might open up. What could this mean for the intuitive mind? I stumbled into something interesting called blindsight phenomena.

In one of my philosophy classes in sixth form, we were exploring different perspectives and the idea that reality is relative. We had a blind girl come in to talk about her experience of life without vision. It was very apparent that she had a strong metaphysical reality. She had lots of spiritual views and referred to herself as a "bit of a witch" in the sense that she was highly intuitive and had her own rituals.

I began to wonder if there was any truth behind the stereotype of blindness being associated with heightened intuition and/or awareness. In films, it's usually the blind person who can see through to other worlds, experiences a connection to the dead, or has supernatural insights, so it's definitely a recognised archetype. Naturally, we are to assume that if one of your senses is taken away, the others are likely to become more acute, and since sight is one of our primary senses, the lack of external stimuli is bound to make us turn inward and connect us to our internal world, but what if it's more than that?

Someone with blindsight is someone who has gone blind who has a form of "second sight." I found a BBC article on second sight that described a man called Daniel.[88] Daniel was half blind. When he had a brain operation to cure his serious headaches, it seemed to have destroyed a region that was crucial for vision. Almost everything to the left of his nose was invisible to him. When Michael Sanders performed some tests on Daniel, something quite piqued his curiosity.

Daniel could reach out and grab Sanders' hand despite the fact that it must have been in his blind spot. There seemed to be a "second sight" guiding his behaviour. Sanders referred Daniel to psychologists Elizabeth Warrington and Lawrence Weiskrantz, who confirmed this hunch with a series of tests. One of the tests they performed involved placing a screen in front of Daniel's blind spot and asking him to point at a circle. Daniel was adamant that he could not see a thing, but Weiskrantz persuaded him to "take a guess." He was almost always right, pointing at the circle around 80 percent of the time, which is phenomenally more than if he was just making lucky guesses.

I took a look into research on pineal gland activity in the blind, and it turns out that due to their loss of vision and lack of feedback from sunlight, the blind suffer with wonky circadian rhythms and melatonin distribution, which can interfere with sleep.[89] So, instead of getting a flood of melatonin (and potentially DMT) at 3:00 to 5:00 a.m.

---

88 David Robson, "Blindsight: The Strangest Form of Consciousness," *BBC*, September 28, 2015, https://www.bbc.com/future/article/20150925-blindsight-the-strangest-form-of-consciousness.

89 Annette E. Allen, "Circadian Rhythms in the Blind," *Current Opinion in Behavioral Sciences* 30 (2019): 73–79, https://doi.org/10.1016/j.cobeha.2019.06.003.

like most people, they are likely to be more dysregulated depending on their level of blindness.[90]

I believe that instead of the more common phenomenon of a 3:00 to 5:00 a.m. window of deep inner awareness, blind people are more likely to be tapped into that creative part of the mind through their waking day-to-day conscious experience.

So what?

So, what about blindsight phenomena and their connections to ancient beliefs and dream state and intuitive phenomena statistics? What does it all actually mean? And what does it mean for you?

These synchronicities imply that intuition peaks when the pineal gland is physically more active. When the pineal gland activity is dysregulated, it appears that intuitive ability can increase throughout the day rather than just in the 3:00 to 5:00 a.m. window at night.

Again, this emphasizes my point that religion and ancient philosophy is a more intuitive way of arriving at truths which not only validate the wisdom of dream states but also show us how far intuition can go.

What if you utilised the wisdom in your dreams and used this 3:00 to 5:00 a.m. window of breakthrough to connect to the deepest parts of yourself, parts that usually never make it to the surface? Surely you would unlock deeper vision and new means of self-mastery.

---

90 Debra J. Skene and Josephine Arendt, "Circadian Rhythm Sleep Disorders in the Blind and Their Treatment with Melatonin," *Sleep Medicine* 8, no. 6 (2007): 651–655, https://doi.org/10.1016/j.sleep.2006.11.013.

How to Communicate with Your Inner Wisdom Through Dream Interpretation

Whatever we can't quite comprehend in words, the mind condenses into symbolic language and pushes to the depths of our subconscious, an aspect of our minds which we have explored through engaging with the imagination in deeper states in meditation. When we learn how to engage with this material and bring it to the surface, we can find keys to deep inner callings and wisdom, but how do we actually find the wisdom in the chaos of our dreams?

Have you ever had a strange dream that feels like nothing more than a meaningless story or vision? Every dream, no matter how strange, has a deeper meaning, and it's up to you to work it out.

Dream interpretation is a good stepping stone for those who are looking for deeper insight into their state of mind but don't feel they are ready for a dedicated meditation practice.

Meditation vs. Dream Interpretation

I would definitely recommend a meditation practice over a dream interpretation practice as it is more lucid and you can control the experience much more.

If you are trying to trigger a specific insight or you have a specific question for which you would like to explore the answer, you can definitely mould the experience a lot more easily through meditation. This is because dreams tend to be a bit more random; but the insights you can get from dreams are still very useful, and it is possible to bring particularly deep insights to the surface.

A meditation practice also improves your chances of dream recall; both of these practices work fantastically hand in hand.

Here are a few tips I use to make sure I don't let any dream content go to waste:

- Keep a dream diary by your bed in easy reach. Write down your dreams the second you are awake before you look at your phone. If you distract yourself before you get to writing, you could easily forget within a matter of minutes. This is also why when I'm working with people in meditations, I get them to write a record of their impressions directly after so that they don't forget their experience.

- If you struggle with dream recall, try a mugwort- or blue-lotus-based tea blend before bed. Mugwort has been used by shamans for centuries for its dream enhancement and intuition enhancing properties. They even used it to enhance astral projection experiences. I created a blend just for this purpose which you can find in my shop, although if you are pregnant, I advise against drinking either mugwort or blue lotus.

- Try not to eat too much of a heavy meal before bed. I was taught that before going into journeying meditations, it's best not to eat at least a few hours before bed. As you digest, your awareness is more focused into the body. I had a hunch that this would apply to sleep and how we experience dream states, and after trial and error I can confirm that it does. Your dreams are definitely going to be more vivid when you go to sleep on a light stomach.

- When you are writing down your dream, make sure to write even the small details that you might not think matter.

- First begin by seeing how the dream as a whole makes you feel and then start to zoom in on the individual components, the storyline, the characters, the scenes, and any kind of other imagery that comes up. Be patient with yourself enough to get how you feel into words and see how this might apply in your life.

- After you have considered how these elements in your dream make you feel on an individual level, you can then explore the archetypal symbolic meanings of your dream symbols by googling or running it through AI software. Just remember that these are guidelines, and how you personally feel about each element of your dreams is more important than the shared definitions.

Lucid Dreaming

If you want to take your dream interpretation practice a step further, you can also work toward something called lucid dreaming.

During the Middle Ages, dreams were often viewed through a religious lens. Christian mystics like St. Augustine and St. Teresa of Ávila described visionary experiences resembling lucid dreams where divine communication occurred in a controlled dream state. These experiences were often reported as taking place in the early morning, aligning with my focus on this time as psychologically significant.

Lucid dreaming is when you are in a dream but are conscious of your actions in the dream; in this state, you can act more autonomously and have control over the environment like in a journeying meditation.[91]

---

91   Ursula Voss and Allan Hobson, "What Is the State-of-the-Art on Lucid Dreaming? Recent Advances and Questions for Future Research," in *Open MIND*, ed. Thomas Metzinger and Jennifer M. Windt (MIT Press, 2015).

These dreams can feel so real it's not uncommon for people to be unable to differentiate lucid dreams from reality.

Other than the great insights, emotional healing, and creative exploration that can take place in a lucid dream, they can also just be a lot of fun. You have the freedom to explore scenarios without any real-world consequences. Lucid dreams can be perfect for rehearsing any actions that you are contemplating or for exploring what certain outcomes might look like.

Although it sounds like a lot of fun, it's important to note that achieving lucidity in dream states requires practice, patience, and mental discipline. Not every attempt will succeed, and in the pursuit of lucid dreaming, you may experience uncomfortable sensations like sleep paralysis.

How to Maximise Your Chances of Lucid Dreaming

Preparation: Maintain a consistent seven-to-nine-hour sleep routine to maximise REM sleep (which peaks 3:00 to 5:00 a.m.). Ensure you are sleeping in a dark, quiet bedroom. Avoid screens one hour before bed and skip heavy meals and caffeine for three to four hours before sleep to enhance dream vividness.

Reality Checks: Reality checks are a cornerstone of lucid dreaming practice because they train your brain to question whether you're awake or dreaming, increasing the likelihood of becoming lucid during a dream.

- Look at text or a clock; recheck it to see if it changes.
- Pinch your nose and try to breathe through it.
- Push a finger through your palm, as it may pass through in dreams.

Mnemonic Induction: Mnemonic induction is a technique to help you become aware that you're dreaming and control your dreams.

- Before bed, repeat to yourself: "I will know I'm dreaming."
- Visualise becoming lucid in a recent dream.

Wake-Back-to-Bed:

- Set an alarm for four to six hours after falling asleep (e.g., for about 3:00 to 4:00 a.m.).
- When the alarm wakes you, stay awake for five to ten minutes, focus on lucid dreaming, then return to sleep.

Meditation to Enhance Awareness:

- Regularly engaging in a simple fifteen-minute awareness meditation practice once per day can significantly improve your chances of being able to experience lucid dreaming.

Managing Sleep Paralysis

As previously mentioned, sleep paralysis is quite likely if you are actively trying to achieve lucid dreaming states, so it is important that you know how to manage these experiences if they do come.

Sleep paralysis is exactly what it sounds like. It's when your mind is awake, but your body is asleep; and sleep paralysis often comes along with vivid sensations and sometimes distressing hallucinations. If this happens, reassure yourself that it is only temporary and is often the breakthrough point to the most vivid lucid dreaming experiences. Try to stay calm when sleep paralysis happens: Focus on your breathing or wiggle your toes to wake up. To enter a lucid dream state from paralysis, visualise a dream scene.

Chapter 6

Women, Children, and Blindsight Phenomena

Diving a little deeper into the mystery of dreams, I made an assumption that those with either higher potential concentrations or greater sensitivity to endogenous DMT in the body would have more vivid dreams, especially with the links to melatonin, circadian rhythms, and the psychedelic nature of particularly vivid dream states.

As someone who has experienced a lot of intuitive phenomena, my dreams are freakishly vivid; and you would assume that if DMT was truly responsible for dream states, then how vivid your dreams are would be determined by either one's sensitivity to DMT or concentration of it.

My dreams are long and vivid, sometimes I even have a few dreams in one night. I have my dream diary from when I was a child, and my dreams really did sound like psychedelic trips. I even experienced lucid dreaming a few times.

So, what if how vivid your dream states are determines how naturally you are able to tune into your intuition? If DMT is linked with intuitive phenomena, and if there are both more intuitive phenomena experiences in dream states and links between dreams and DMT, then our dreams would be a logical place to look to see how tuned in or tuned out you are to your intuitive wisdom.

Women's Intuition

When you think of intuition as a mainstream topic, perhaps you think of women's intuition. Scientifically and culturally, it seems that women tend to be more intuitive than men. In many spiritual traditions, intuition is associated with the feminine, and "women's intuition" as well as "mothers' intuition" both seem to be quite well-known terms.

The scientific revolution elevated rationalism and empiricism while discarding subjective knowing. Intuition was relegated to the realm of superstition or "feminine emotionality." Women were therefore excluded from scientific institutions and philosophical debates, as they were seen as too emotional for "objective thought." Carl Jung noted that intuition was more predominant in women.

Women's Dreams vs. Men's Dreams

In theory, women's dreams should be more vivid. As it turns out, women's dreams are much more abstract than men's dreams; and not only this, but women are reported to dream more often than men and can remember their dreams more easily.[92,93]

---

92 G. W. Domhoff, "The Dreams of Men and Women: Patterns of Gender Similarity and Difference" (University of California, Santa Cruz, 2005), https://dreams.ucsc.edu/Library/domhoff_2005c.html.

93 Michael Schredl and Iris Reinhard, "Gender Differences in Dream Recall: A Meta Analysis," *Journal of Sleep Research* 17, no. 2 (2008): 125–131, https://doi.org/10.1111/j.1365-2869.2008.00626.x.

I began reflecting: What traits that make up the feminine woman and differ from the masculine could possibly help us to understand women's intuition and the nature of intuition and consciousness?

Women Tend to Be...

MORE EMPATHETIC

Simon Baron-Cohen's theory of empathizing vs. systemizing suggests that women are more likely to "empathize" (understand the world through people and feelings), while men more often "systemize" (analyse systems and rules).[94]

MORE CREATIVE IN THEIR EXPRESSION

Think about men's fashion compared to women's, or even their home decor choices. Women tend to be more expressive in their aesthetics; men on the other hand may lean more toward minimalism and practicality.[95]

MORE EMOTIONAL

This has been consistently supported by research across neuroscience, endocrinology, developmental psychology, and emotional intelligence studies.[96]

---

94   Simon Baron-Cohen, "Autism: The Empathizing-Systemizing (E-S) Theory," *The Year in Cognitive Neuroscience 2009* 1156, no. 1 (2009): 68–80, https://doi.org/10.1111/j.1749-6632.2009.04467.x.

95   Cathy Bakewell and Vincent-Wayne Mitchell, "Male Versus Female Consumer Decision Making Styles," *Journal of Business Research* 59, no. 12 (2006): 1297–1300, https://doi.org/10.1016/j.jbusres.2006.09.008.

96   John Brebner, "Gender and Emotions," *Personality and Individual Differences 34*, no. 3 (2003): 387–394, https://doi.org/10.1016/S0191-8869(02)00059-4.

This got me thinking in terms of DMT in the body. I would hypothesise that women would have more DMT in their systems or a heightened sensitivity to it due to what is shown by these factors of intuition and dream states alone. But here is where things get interesting—because when people take psychedelics, do they not become more empathetic and in tune with their feelings?

Women's Intuition and Psychedelic Psychology

A 2024 meta-analysis of certain psychedelics—LSD, psilocybin, and ayahuasca—using the Multifaceted Empathy Test found that these substances significantly boost explicit and implicit emotional empathy.[97]

Psychedelics have been known as creative stimulants used by artists to boost the creative process. One study on ayahuasca showed that it boosts your capacity for creative thinking.[98] Psilocybin has shown similar results; in an international study, researchers found it enhanced creative thinking overall, not just in the moment but for weeks after a psilocybin experience.[99] This isn't new knowledge, either. As far back as the mid-twentieth century, researchers exploring LSD were already observing

---

97 Amit Olami and Leehe Peled-Avron, "Effects of Classical Psychedelics on Implicit and Explicit Emotional Empathy and Cognitive Empathy: A Meta-Analysis of MET Task," *Scientific Reports* 14 (2024), https://doi.org/10.1038/s41598-024-74810-w.

98 K. P. C. Kuypers et al., "Ayahuasca Enhances Creative Divergent Thinking While Decreasing Conventional Convergent Thinking," *Psychopharmacology* 233 (2016): 3395–3403, https://doi.org/10.1007/s00213-016-4377-8.

99 Natasha L. Mason et al., "Sub-Acute Effects of Psilocybin on Empathy, Creative Thinking, and Subjective Well-Being," *Journal of Psychoactive Drugs* 51, no. 2 (2019): 123–134, https://doi.org/10.1080/02791072.2019.1580804.

heightened creativity, especially in artists and problem-solvers.[100] There's a long-standing connection between psychedelics and creative intelligence.

Don't psychedelics often profoundly enhance emotional sensitivity?

Psychedelics appear to amplify emotional sensitivity and openness by modulating brain networks related to self-referential thought and social cognition. This can lead to enhanced emotional states.[101]

It was clear to me that I had to do some research into the pineal gland in women and into melatonin production in the female body to see if there was a biological difference that would make sense of the differences in women's and men's experiences.

It turns out that circadian rhythm studies show that women generally produce more melatonin at night and that it peaks earlier in their daily cycle compared to men. Women's melatonin cycles are often more sensitive to light, meaning that they may experience stronger melatonin production in response to darkness.[102]

If this is not enough, it turns out that several other studies have shown that testosterone, which is present in men in significantly higher quantities than women, can suppress melatonin production in the pineal gland. This means higher levels of testosterone may be linked to lower melatonin levels and therefore may potentially be connected to lower DMT levels.[103]

That's women's intuition, but who else may be having intuitive experiences?

---

[100] Isabel Wießner et al., "LSD and Creativity: Increased Novelty and Symbolic Thinking, Decreased Utility and Convergent Thinking," *Journal of Psychopharmacology* 36, no. 3 (2022), https://doi.org/10.1177/02698811211069113.

[101] F. Moujaes et al., "The Emotional Architecture of the Psychedelic Brain," *Trends in Cognitive Sciences* 29, no. 11 (2025): 1007–1022, https://doi.org/10.1016/j.tics.2025.07.006.

[102] Parisa Vidafar et al., "Greater Sensitivity of the Circadian System of Women to Bright Light, but Not Dim to Moderate Light," *Journal of Pineal Research* 76, no. 2 (2024): e12936, https://doi.org/10.1111/jpi.12936.

[103] Anna Werrett, "The Effects of Melatonin on Testosterone Levels: What You Need to Know," MedShun, January 21, 2024, https://medshun.com/article/does-melatonin-affect-testosterone.

Children's Intuition

I once saw a post on Instagram where there was a toddler wobbling around with a confused look on his face, and the caption was, "Why do toddlers act like they are on psychedelics all the time?" It made me giggle, but I thought to myself, "Wait…they *could* actually be on psychedelics all the time!"

Children are highly intuitive, and I have heard many stories from people who claimed to have had intuitive gifts or to have experienced intuitive phenomena as a child and said that as they grew older, they found it more difficult to connect intuitively or didn't have as many of these experiences.

In supernatural films, it is often the child that somehow has this special connection to the other side that the grown-ups don't quite understand. I don't feel like this is too far from the truth.

I had the most potent and regular intuitive experiences when I was younger. My dad also had most of his mystical experiences when he was younger, as did many of my other friends and family members with whom I have discussed intuitive phenomena.

In several spiritual traditions, it is believed that children have more of a connection with the unseen.

Indigo Children

In new age spirituality, the phrase "indigo children" is used to describe children who are believed to possess special, unusual, and sometimes supernatural traits or abilities.

The idea is based on concepts developed in the seventies by Nancy Ann Tappe, who claimed to be noticing indigo children in the late sixties. These children are believed to have high intelligence and healing abilities, as well as heightened empathy and creativity.

A study for "indigo children" was done with adults who grew up with this intuitive phenomenon. The study that was performed revealed that as intuitive children, the ten subjects all revealed similar themes in personal interviews that explored their backgrounds. The primary findings drawn from these interviews were that the grandmother or mother had a similar gift, they often felt misunderstood, and they often had a history of abuse and violence or were frequently disciplined, which again builds on the idea of trauma as a stimulant to DMT production discussed in Chapter 4.[104] It was concluded that these children felt mislabelled or misunderstood throughout their lives. Neale Donald Walsch stated, "Indigo children have access to human experience at a larger level, at a greater depth than most people do."[105]

Native American Beliefs

Some Native American tribes also believe children are closer to the spirit world due to their recent arrival from it. Children who see spirits or have vivid dreams are often seen as having "medicine gifts."

Taoist Beliefs

In Chinese Taoism, children are believed to be born in harmony with "the Tao," and those with psychic sight or energetic sensitivity may be

---

[104] Lulu Bagnol et al., "Indigos in Hawaii: A Phenomenological Study of the Experience of Growing Up with Spiritual Intelligence," *Pacific Health Dialog* 17, no. 1 (2011): 83–98, https://pubmed.ncbi.nlm.nih.gov/23008973.

[105] "So-Called Indigo Teen Says She Can Read People," ABC News, July 25, 2006, https://abcnews.go.com/GMA/AmericanFamily/story?id=2224795&page=1.

trained in *qigong* or spiritual arts. Dreams and visions in childhood are often taken seriously, especially if they involve ancestors.

So here is a take that many people and schools of thought have been intuitively connecting to, but is there anything that backs these intuitions?

Pineal Gland Activity and Melatonin Production in Children

According to my theory, the pineal gland in children should therefore either be bigger or more active.

As expected, melatonin levels are highest in children aged two to three. During the remainder of childhood, melatonin levels drop progressively by 50–60 percent. As we enter adulthood, our melatonin drops by another 30 percent.[106]

Children not only dream significantly more vividly than adults, but there is a significant increase in reported lucid dreaming in children.[107]

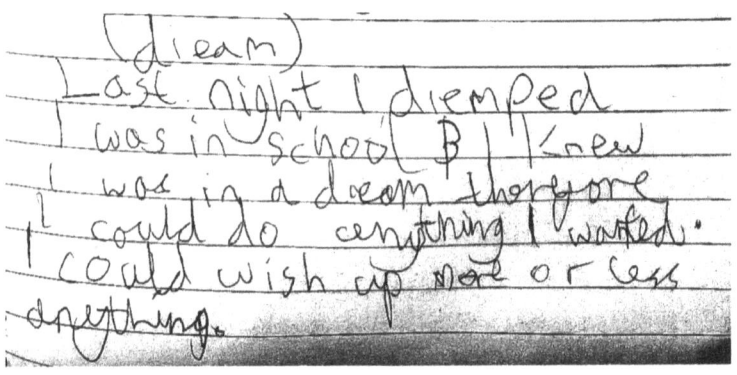

106 Julio Ardura et al., "Emergence and Evolution of the Circadian Rhythm of Melatonin in Children," *Hormone Research in Paediatrics* 59, no. 2 (2003): 66–72, https://doi.org/10.1159/000068571.

107 Ursula Voss et al., "Lucid Dreaming: An Age-Dependent Brain Dissociation," *Journal of Sleep Research* 21, no. 6 (2012): 634–642, https://doi.org/10.1111/j.1365-2869.2012.01022.x.

This is an extract from my childhood diary from when I was eight to nine years old which shows that I was lucid dreaming. I remember this is something that I experienced a few times.

Jung believed that there was a deep wisdom in children's dreams. From his perspective, children are capable of greater insight into the collective unconscious. He believed children's dreams show profound truths by means of archetypal symbols. Jung explained:

> *"The dreams of children are often extremely vivid, and their contents sometimes strikingly profound and wise, as though the child had access to a deeper layer of reality than we expect."*[108]
>
> —C. G. Jung, *The Collected Works of C. G. Jung, Volume 9 (Part I): The Archetypes and the Collective Unconscious*

Children's Imagination and Creativity

I went to visit family friends of my dad, a couple who had a six-year-old daughter called Eden. She had artworks all over the walls, and I was struck by their similarity to psychedelic art styles.

She told me one piece in particular was titled "Night Time." When most people think of the night, they think of the dark; but in her interpretation, there was incredible colour. The sky was purple and there were multicoloured clouds. There was a street where each house was a

---

[108] Carl G. Jung, *The Collected Works of C. G. Jung, Volume 9 (Part I): The Archetypes and the Collective Unconscious*, ed. and trans. Gerhard Adler and R. F. C. Hull (Princeton University Press, 1969).

different colour, and there were flowers and animals everywhere. That is how Eden saw the world: creatively full of colour. The same often applies for other children too; it's like they view the world with a technicolour lens.

I feel like at some point in our lives we all have the distinct feeling that life does not look the same as it did when we were kids—that things are not as colourful and vibrant as they used to be.

What if children *literally* view the world as more colourful?

As we get older, our perception of colour fades, which is why, seen through an adult lens, the world does not look the same as when we were kids.[109] I wondered if this could be something to do with DMT or the pineal gland because psychology says that psychedelics have profound effects on colour perception, and it has even been speculated psychedelics can improve colour blindness.[110]

Like properties that show up in psychedelic psychology, children also tend to be:[111,112,113]

- More emotional
- More intuitive
- More creative

---

[109] "Color Vision Problems Become More Common with Age, Study Shows," *ScienceDaily*, February 24, 2014, https://www.sciencedaily.com/releases/2014/02/140220102614.htm.

[110] J. E. C. Anthony et al., "Improved Colour Blindness Symptoms Associated with Recreational Psychedelic Use: Results from the Global Drug Survey 2017," *Drug Science, Policy and Law* 6 (2020), https://doi.org/10.1177/2050324520942345.

[111] Jack P. Shonkoff et al., "Children's Emotional Development Is Built into the Architecture of Their Brains," Working Paper No. 2 (Center on the Developing Child, Harvard University, August 2011), https://harvardcenter.wpenginepowered.com/wp-content/uploads/2004/04/Childrens-Emotional-Development-Is-Built-Into-the-Architecture-of-Their-Brains.pdf.

[112] Joshua A. Confer et al., "Children and Adults' Intuitions of What People Can Believe," *Child Development* 95, no. 2 (2024): 447–461, https://doi.org/10.1111/cdev.13988.

[113] Alison Gopnik et al., "Changes in Cognitive Flexibility and Hypothesis Search across Human Life History from Childhood to Adolescence to Adulthood," *Proceedings of the National Academy of Sciences* 114, no. 30 (2017): 7892–7899, https://doi.org/10.1073/pnas.1700811114.

To test the idea that children are more intuitive, I decided to do some tests on my younger cousin Blake when he was around ten years old to see just how far children's intuition could go.

Blake was a very creative child who loved to draw, dance, and play music, so I was eager to see if his intuition would match.

To test out his intuition, I thought I would dig into my crystal collection and pick out some different coloured stones to see how he would respond to each one. Perhaps not the most scientific method, but I was really into crystals at the time, and even something like alignments to the colour psychology properties of each crystal would be something.

I had noticed that the metaphysical properties of crystals often aligned with the colour of the crystal and colour psychology. For example, green and gold crystals often symbolised abundance, purple crystals symbolised creativity and intuition, and yellow crystals symbolised joy and energy, the same as in colour psychology. So, if what he felt and the corresponding metaphysical properties to each crystal matched, it would at least mean something in this sense even if you can't connect to the idea of the metaphysical properties of crystals.

I guided him through some basic meditation exercises before handing him each crystal one at a time and asking, "If this crystal had the power to make you feel anything in the world, what would it be?"

The first crystal that I gave him was chrysoprase. Chrysoprase is a light aqua colour, and its properties are calming and soothing. When I placed this crystal in his hand, he said, "I feel like I am flying in the sky, mindfulness realm, like you are the rock, like the rock is the sky and you are inside the rock, like you were in some other calm world."

I was quite shocked.

That is in theory how chrysoprase should make you feel based on its metaphysical description, and he said it without hesitating. The rest of the crystal descriptions were just as symbolic, abstract, graphic, and just as accurate.

TIGER'S EYE

Properties: Tiger's eye is well-known as the crystal used for courage and to settle anxiety. It is a stone of protection and strength.

Blake's description: "Like you are above everything, like you are feeling out of this world."

TOFFEE JASPER

Properties: The properties of toffee jasper are massively grounding. It's supposed to make you feel more grounded and stable when you focus on it in meditation.

Blake's description: "Like you are not in above the sky, like muddy, steady like stuck somewhere, like you can move but you don't want to."

ROSE QUARTZ

Properties: Emotional soothing, inner peace, and heart healing.

Blake's description: "A dimension where there are pink clouds in the sky, but pink clouds are all there is, it feels comforting, calm, friendly."

BLACK OBSIDIAN

Properties: Protection against negativity. It draws out mental stress and stimulates growth.

Blake's description: "Feels deep and dark like before time."

I thought that I would take things a step further by blindfolding him and see what came up. This time I included different tumbled stones that he hadn't seen before, just in case he had memorised the slight size and shape differences.

He was either completely correct or close in describing the first five, then when I told him he was getting them right, his answers went off; but all in all, he displayed great intuitive ability.

Stories of Children's Intuition

Francesca McCartney, PhD, spoke about the phenomena of highly intuitive children. As a former Montessori teacher, she said she heard many intuitively insightful comments from her young students. "What is your baby's name?" one six-year-old said to her teacher. No adult in the school knew that this teacher was pregnant.

The mother of one of her students reported that she was driving down a winding road when her four-year-old daughter made a perplexing statement: "Mommy, how did the deer die?" As the mother turned the corner, a dead deer lay on the road. She arrived at the preschool classroom to drop off her daughter shaken by the incident and a little fearful of her daughter's perception.

Why Are Children More Intuitive and Creative than Adults?

I took another look into the biology of the pineal gland and psychology in children as opposed to adults to see if there is anything more than melatonin production to give us insight into children's intuition, and I found some factors that provide us more context.

Pineal Gland Size

First of all, when a child is born, its pineal gland is actually larger than it is in adults. The pineal gland grows in size from birth until around two years of age, and then it remains relatively stable in size from two to twenty years old. After puberty, the pineal gland tends to shrink.[114]

Layers of Experience

It is undeniable that as we grow older, we grow layers—layers of experience that grow our understanding. But these layers of experience, although they add to our understanding, also make it naturally more difficult to connect to the purer expression of consciousness we are all born with before we are shaped by our environment and societal norms.

Think of your mind as being like the inside of a tree trunk that grows layers as we age.

Children process the world a lot more intuitively before they have the conscious information to build up their understanding.

Pineal Gland Calcification

As you get older, without conscious maintenance, your pineal gland calcifies.[115]

This means that there is a higher risk of decreased pineal gland activity, which is also linked to brain health illnesses such as Alzheimer's. As we age, calcium deposits begin to naturally accumulate

---

[114] M. Sumida et al., "Development of the Pineal Gland: Measurement with MR," *American Journal of Neuroradiology* 17, no. 2 (1996): 233–236, https://www.ajnr.org/content/17/2/233.short.

[115] "What to Know About Calcification of the Pineal Gland," *WebMD*, October 16, 2024, https://www.webmd.com/sleep-disorders/what-to-know-about-calcification-of-the-pineal-gland.

in the pineal gland. This is especially common in industrialized countries due to fluoride exposure, poor diet, lack of sunlight, and environmental toxins. The gland essentially becomes coated in calcium crystals, which hardens it and interferes with its ability to produce melatonin and possibly other neuromodulators.[116]

How You Can Prevent Pineal Gland Calcification

- Decrease fluoride intake by drinking more filtered or spring water and switching from fluoride toothpastes to fluoride-free products.[117]

- Support decalcification with natural chelators, including:

  1. **Boron:** Helps detox fluoride. Can be found in prunes and avocados.[118]

  2. **Tamarind:** This fruit has been shown to help flush fluoride from the body.[119]

  3. **Calcium:** Reduces fluoride absorption.[120]

---

116 Dun X. Tan et al., "Pineal Calcification, Melatonin Production, Aging, Associated Health Consequences and Rejuvenation of the Pineal Gland," *Molecules* 23, no. 2 (2018): 301, https://doi.org/10.3390/molecules23020301.

117 Jennifer A. Luke, "The Effect of Fluoride on the Physiology of the Pineal Gland" (PhD diss., University of Surrey, 1997), https://openresearch.surrey.ac.uk/esploro/outputs/doctoral/The-Effect-of-Fluoride-on-the/99516257402346.

118 V. Bhuti, "Boron as an Antidote to Fluoride Toxicity," *Epidemiology* 18, no. 5 (2007): S109–S110, https://doi.org/10.1097/01.ede.0000288441.02944.26.

119 A. L. Khandare et al., "Effect of Tamarind Ingestion on Fluoride Excretion in Humans," *European Journal of Clinical Nutrition* 56 (2002): 82–85, https://doi.org/10.1038/sj.ejcn.1601287.

120 Herta Spencer et al., "Effect of Sodium Fluoride on Calcium Absorption and Balances in Man," *The American Journal of Clinical Nutrition* 22, no. 4 (1969): 381–390, https://doi.org/10.1093/ajcn/22.4.381.

Chapter 7

The Creative Nature of Consciousness

◆◆

Links Between Creativity and Potential DMT Production

On the topic of creativity, it's interesting to note that psychedelics have been used to consciously enhance creative thinking for almost as long as they have been around.

Many scientific studies have also now confirmed that psychedelics can be used to enhance creative thinking. A study by Natasha Mason investigated the effects of psilocybin on creativity in a trial with fifty-five healthy participants.[121]

The study assessed divergent thinking and convergent thinking using activities like the Picture Concept Task. Participants were able

---

121 Natasha L. Mason et al., "Sub-Acute Effects of Psilocybin on Empathy, Creative Thinking, and Subjective Well-Being," *Journal of Psychoactive Drugs* 51, no. 2 (2019): 123–134, https://doi.org/10.1080/02791 072.2019.1580804.

to come up with more associations, with higher originality, between pictures that they were shown the morning after taking psilocybin.

Many musicians and artists have been known to use psychedelics for creativity; the Beatles famously came up with some of their best works under their influence. Works such as those of Beaumont and the Romanian painter Michăilescu take the viewer to extremely abstract territories inspired by psychedelic trips. Scientists have also enhanced their creativity with psychedelics.

But to reemphasise a key point, you don't need to reach for anything outside of yourself for this creativity. You can reach these states naturally in a controlled and healthy way with meditations. You can do psychedelic therapy for free, with no external psychedelics and in the comfort of your own home.

The Unconscious and Its Links to Creativity

As people we can have different sizes of consciousness, this just means the extent of our awareness can vary from person to person.

The size of your consciousness and the quality of your awareness determine the depth of your intuition, according to Jungian psychology.

Jung believed that the more you integrate your unconscious into conscious awareness (which basically just means finding ways to put your feelings into words or rather a tangible form), the more access to deeper symbolic and intuitive material you have, which makes for great creative ability. Due to the shared nature of what we experience in the depths of our minds, the more that you are able to identify and bring to the surface deep unconscious material, the more deeply other people will be able to connect with it.

Perhaps they won't even know why they connect with it so deeply; but this unknowing occurs because they have not yet brought to the surface the deep part of themselves that identifies with what you have created. It becomes a deep inner calling, and this also gives depth to why so many people connect so deeply to religions and ancient forms of spirituality that contain a lot of deeply archetypal symbols and material.

Despite the archetypal awareness, there are many other factors that affect how practices like meditation increase creativity through inner experience and through expanding the awareness. Creativity and creative ability seem to increase with intuitive ability.

Connecting to Inspiration

All great vision starts off with a creative spark. True inspiration is something that is found deep within us. When you get that sudden glimpse of inspiration, it feels like an alignment and is something that feels exciting to express or explore.

When you bring your awareness deep within yourself, you are more likely to find deeper alignments in things and therefore see more fulfilling or exciting causes of action.

When you live a life attuned to inspiration, things become more vibrant and meaningful. Life becomes more filled with wonder and possibility.

You become open to a direct channel of inspiration when you are more connected to your intuition. Ideas flow more naturally and creativity feels more effortless.

I have noticed that artists, creatives, and inventors are usually highly intuitive people and seem to have greater spiritual or introspective inclinations than most. I believe that understanding the chaotic nature of creativity and consciousness can also give you more insight into this topic.

Creativity, Chaos, and Consciousness from the Cosmos to the Quantum

"you need chaos in your soul to give birth to a dancing star"
—Friedrich Nietzsche [122]

Understanding the relationship between chaos, consciousness, and creativity from a metaphysical point of view brings intriguing insight to what it might look like psychologically to expand our awareness by bringing our awareness inwards. This understanding builds bridges to comprehension of the potential role of psychedelics in the body and how meditation helps us tap into that to enhance our imaginative and intuitive ability.

It's not just chaos in the mind that induces creativity; it does so literally on every scale. The Big Bang and the creation of the universe is one of the best examples. The Big Bang created the universe in a state of chaos.

When we zoom into physical matter to the highest degree, where things get very, very small, we come across quantum particles. Quantum physics is very chaotic. It has driven physicists mad as long as it has been around. It is from this perceived chaos that things form.

---

122   Friedrich Nietzsche, *Thus Spoke Zarathustra*, trans. Walter Kaufmann (Modern Library, 1995).

You can say that it is enough to state that everything physically in existence is born from chaos, but what about metaphysically? New ideas? Visions?

The more conscious a life form seems to be, the more complex its life seems to be, the more chaos there is, and the more it can perceive and see order in more complex and chaotic systems.[123] The lives and knowledge of higher conscious life forms can only be perceived as chaos by lesser conscious life forms.[124]

"the ability to see order in chaos is called Creativity" - Simon Sinek[125]

Let's talk about the chaos and creativity connection.

So, first of all, how do we define creativity? Creativity is the urge to make, build, and express. It's what helps us to solve problems and foresee possibilities. To be alive is to create, we are constantly stepping into a new vision. I believe that life is one big creative act in this sense and that creativity is a life force of sorts. Creativity becomes a mirror of inner experience and perception: All things that we create first start as something within us, something that starts as a feeling and finds its form as an idea or vision.

---

123 James P. Crutchfield, "Between Order and Chaos," *Nature Physics* 8 (2012): 17–24, https://doi.org/10.1038/nphys2190.

124 Robert Lawrence Kuhn, "A Landscape of Consciousness: Toward a Taxonomy of Explanations and Implications," *Progress in Biophysics and Molecular Biology* 190 (2024): 28–169, https://doi.org/10.1016/j.pbiomolbio.2023.12.003.

125 Simon Sinek, "Love Your Work," hosted by Tina Roth Eisenberg, posted April 20, 2012, by CreativeMornings, video, 42 min., 8 sec., https://creativemornings.com/talks/simon-sinek.

The more conscious you are, the more creative you can be because you are drawing from a richer inner world.

There is this stereotype of the chaotic artist or the mad scientist. My definition of a creative is not just in the artsy, aesthetic design sense. I believe that we are all inherently creative; when we process or bring our vision of anything into existence, I see that as a creative act.

It figures that those I see as great creatives are people with a strong sense of vision and the ability to bring that vision into existence.

Chaotic Creatives and Inventors in History

Throughout history, the best creatives and the most phenomenal minds seem to come from great chaos one way or another.

One of the best examples of how chaos and creativity go hand in hand in terms of psychology is Tesla.

Nikola Tesla was one of the greatest geniuses who ever lived. Known as the grandfather of electricity and a talented visionary, his discoveries and inventions are fundamental to the modern reality that we exist in today.

Tesla, who was often described as mad, had many quirks that set him apart from most people. He had an obsession with the number three and used to do his tasks in sets of three; he would ask to be booked into hotel rooms with numbers divisible by three. He also had an intense phobia of pearls, to the extent that he would refuse to speak to women wearing them, and he had a soft spot for pigeons, particularly one white pigeon. He even claimed that this pigeon communicated with him and reportedly said that he felt he received inspiration from her. Could these quirks be the manifestation of the very same chaos within Tesla that contributed to his genius?

When coming up with his inventions, Tesla would not always build his prototypes of his inventions by piecing them together logically bit by bit; he would sometimes describe his inventions to come as flash visions fully formed in his mind, complete with mathematical equations and mechanical designs which he would then build. He claimed to see these ideas in his head as vividly as if they were real, and once the thought came to him, he had to act on it immediately. He was certainly not the only creative who made waves in history with notable quirks or who had experienced some sort of catalytic chaos at some point in their lives. In fact, I find this is the case with almost all of them.

Leonardo da Vinci also famously described being able to see objects in his mind and rotate them in full three dimensions before drawing or building them.

This kind of visionary ability sounds almost identical to the concept of "intuitive downloads," a term used to describe when we are suddenly inexplicably flooded with intuitive insights and visions.

The phrase "intuitive download" or the concept of unexplainable yet insightful visions may sound mystical at first, but here you see they are woven into the very fabric that built the world that we live in today.

How This Shows Up in History

Even in history it can be shown that the greatest periods of innovation have emerged from periods of great destruction. The Renaissance, for example, is the time period when great creative minds such as Michelangelo and Leonardo da Vinci made their contributions.

Historian Bernd Roeck said: "There is probably no place in the world where so much was discussed in one big conversation involving such a large number of participants, where things were invented in such quick succession than the Renaissance."[126]

The Renaissance, one of the most innovative and creative periods in history, followed directly after one of the most destructive and chaotic periods in history—the Black Death. The intense chaos and destruction brought on by this pandemic wiped out a shocking 60 percent of Europe's population.

So often, people romanticize the beauty and the genius of Renaissance art and architecture, but there would have been no Renaissance without its shadow. Many people forget that the Renaissance in itself isn't the full picture.

I decided to do a little digging into the psychology and neuroscience of chaos and creativity.

The Neuroscience of Chaos and Creation

In the field of neuroscience, I learned about a state called "criticality." Criticality refers to a theoretical state of the brain or neural networks that lies at the edge between order and chaos, often called the critical point, a concept borrowed from physics and complex systems.[127]

Creative cognition was linked to a brain that hovers near criticality, enabling network flexibility and rich mental simulation.[128]

---

[126] "The Renaissance: The Age of Michelangelo and Leonardo Da Vinci (1/2)," posted April 28, 2019, by DW Documentary, YouTube, 42 min., 25 sec., https://www.youtube.com/watch?v=BmHTQsxxkPk.

[127] Yang Tian et al., "Theoretical Foundations of Studying Criticality in the Brain," *Network Neuroscience* 6, no. 4 (2022): 1148–1185, https://doi.org/10.1162/netn_a_00269.

[128] "The Neuroscience of Creativity and 'Aha!' Moments," *Science News Today*, August 8, 2025, https://www.sciencenewstoday.org/the-neuroscience-of-creativity-and-aha-moments.

In a state of criticality, the brain shows evidence of these characteristics:[129]

- More flexible associations
- Greater variability in brain activity
- Higher responsiveness to stimuli

All of the above support creative thinking.

States of chaos help us connect to ideas that are perhaps more unconventional, bypassing habitual thought loops. When we ground these ideas in our understanding by finding the order in the chaos, we create something new. We find new insights into things, come up with new ideas, and bring new creation into the world.

Criticality is when neural activity hovers on the edge between stability and unpredictability: not too rigid but not too random. At this edge, the brain becomes highly sensitive and able to spot patterns, connect ideas, and respond intuitively.[130]

This "edge of chaos" is where creative insights, intuition, and breakthroughs often happen.

It reminds me a lot of an art practice I remember doing in primary school. We were taught to take a pencil and scribble random lines on a piece of paper and then later try to add to it by finding constellations and building on these chaotic scribbles, using pen and paint to create pieces of art. What was at first just a scribble on a page in pencil could become a peacock, a vase, a slice of cake, or whatever the student saw, as far as the imagination might reach. This could include original ideas

---

129 Minkyung Kim et al., "Criticality Creates a Functional Platform for Network Transitions Between Internal and External Processing Modes in the Human Brain," *Frontiers in Systems Neuroscience* 15 (2021), https://doi.org/10.3389/fnsys.2021.657809.

130 Minkyung Kim et al., "Criticality Creates a Functional Platform for Network Transitions Between Internal and External Processing Modes in the Human Brain," *Frontiers in Systems Neuroscience* 15 (2021), https://doi.org/10.3389/fnsys.2021.657809.

that you would not have been able to come up with if you were simply told to just paint whatever it is you imagined you should paint.

We will again explore the esoteric and historic schools of thought that relate to chaos and creativity. I find that when it comes to the topic of intuition and metaphysics in general, it's interesting to look back as the ancients had undeniable wisdom and likely had a deeper experience of the self as a result of their environment and resulting cultures, as previously explored in Chapter 3.

Esoteric and Philosophical Interpretations of Chaos and Creation

Ego Death

In many spiritual traditions, there is the concept of ego death, in which you supposedly reach deeper layers of understanding of yourself and the universe, allowing the possibility of expanding your consciousness beyond your everyday personality. It is said that your ego can in some ways blind you to seeing deeper truths by keeping our level of consciousness focused on a limited scope of attention. Certainty can blind us, but when our ego is broken down, we may break through to new perspectives, therefore expanding our awareness and deepening our intuitive ability.

Ego death is said to feel chaotic to experience. When everything we think we know changes or we suddenly see things from a new angle that fundamentally shifts how we view the world, there is always uncertainty. It's this chaos which is the price of growth and change.

Alchemy

Alchemy is an ancient philosophical and proto-scientific tradition that aimed to transform, purify, and perfect both matter and the human soul. It has been described as the spiritual ancestor of modern chemistry since its primary objective was to turn base metals like lead into gold. It was performed in a ritualistic setting, and each step in the process had a deeply symbolic meaning.

In alchemy, there is a goal which reflects the idea that clarity found in chaos is a somewhat magical process by which we are able to expand our awareness and develop deeper wisdom and intuitive knowledge. This was traditionally called alchemical transmutation, and it involved a few symbolic stages that were each performed in a ritual setting.

Jung also believed that these alchemical stages reflected the process of "individuation," which is a Jungian term used to describe becoming whole. Individuation enables us to act more in alignment to the deeper aspects of the self and connect more deeply to our intuition. Here are the stages so you can see how they reflect the mental process of developing wisdom through chaos.

The Symbolic Stages of Alchemical Transmutation

CALCINATION (BURNING AWAY THE FALSE SELF)

This represents breaking down the ego, pride, and false beliefs. It's the beginning of transformation, during which illusions are destroyed by inner or outer fire.

DISSOLUTION (MELTING WHAT REMAINS)

Old structures melt. Emotions and the unconscious rise to the surface. It's a time of confusion, but also of deep emotional release.

SEPARATION (SORTING THE PURE FROM THE IMPURE)

You begin to see clearly. Truth is separated from illusion. This is where intuition first sharpens, and you start to know what's truly you.

CONJUNCTION (UNITING OPPOSITES)

The conscious and unconscious mind begin to work together. Masculine and feminine, logic and feeling, shadow and light find balance.

FERMENTATION (A SPARK OF NEW LIFE)

This is the start of spiritual rebirth. A higher awareness or intuitive vision begins to awaken. You glimpse something beyond ordinary reality.

DISTILLATION (REFINING THE SPIRIT)

Consciousness is refined. Meditation, insight, and clarity deepen. Intuition becomes pure and reliable.

COAGULATION: THE PHILOSOPHER'S STONE (BECOMING WHOLE)

The Self is realised. Intuition, soul, and mind are aligned. You are no longer divided, you are whole, wise, and creatively empowered.

I find alchemy a deeply fascinating practice, having found that many ancient practices or rituals reflect almost intuitive forms of psychotherapy.

"In all chaos there is a cosmos, In all disorder, a secret order"
— Jung [131]

---

131 Carl G. Jung, *The Collected Works of C. G. Jung, Volume 9 (Part I): The Archetypes and the Collective Unconscious*, ed. and trans. Gerhard Adler and R. F. C. Hull (Princeton University Press, 1969).

How This Can Show Up in Your Life

I have noticed the wisdom of chaos and creation playing out in my own life many times. When reading through all my diary entries, I noticed that in periods where I was generally more content, my extracts were more perky, but they were also simpler. In the most difficult and chaotic periods of my life, however, I found that I had more ideas for paintings and blogs as well as more questions that I explored, and generally there was a lot more richness in my writing.

Don't get me wrong; I am by no means trying to glorify or promote chaos and disorder, but I want to provide a light at the end of the tunnel for anyone who feels they are in a particularly difficult or chaotic period of their lives. The stressful uncertainty that comes with chaos is like alchemical gold when you know how to manage it.

Trust the Wisdom in Chaos

Trust the wisdom in chaos even if you can't immediately see that change is happening. You must trust that when the light comes back, you will be able to see everything that you have built in the dark, and you will then be able to lean on it. Enjoy a life enriched with new realisations and remind yourself that when you find yourself in a dark place again, it's never all darkness when you really understand how much opportunity and potential it can bring you.

Finding Clarity in the Chaos

Chaos isn't this amazing creative force just in itself; chaos without the ability to slow down enough to see order in it is only chaos. Not everyone sits with how they feel long enough to find clarity in the chaos of their emotions. It's necessary to be patient with the process in order to bring intuitive wisdom to the surface; this is why it often remains unconscious.

This is why I feel so passionate about making more conscious efforts to slow down in a world that only seems to get faster and more distracting. A fast-paced routine and media consumption can not only stagnate the natural mental healing process but also tend to hold back great potential.

As mentioned in previous chapters, the key is this process of being still and focused enough to see the order in the chaos. When we have found it, life opens up to us. This is the active process of breaking through to the deeper insight to which you have been called.

To be able to sit with how you feel without trying to distract yourself takes trust. You might feel irritated and anxious when you are consumed by the uncertainty of change, unpredictability, or chaotic periods in your life.

It feels counterintuitive to sit and "do nothing." The wonderful thing about your mind is that it is ever evolving, and whatever you bring awareness to evolves as you do even if it might not always immediately feel that way. How we feel always shifts moment to moment.

I can tell you this, and you might understand it logically, but if you have not yet *felt* the transformation, it's more difficult to connect to it.

Meditation and introspection are uncomfortable at first, especially when you are in periods of chaos, so it's really important that you trust the process until the real life-changing transformation has a chance to take place.

How Does Meditation Enhance Creativity and the Ability to Give Form to Our Feelings?

Meditation enhances creativity in a number of ways. With experience, it becomes undeniable that meditation is the best practice to increase creative thinking.

Stress Reduction

On a basic level, meditation reduces stress, which helps your creative mind to emerge.[132] When you are stressed out, you find it difficult to think creatively because you are in survival mode. So, when meditation helps you to regulate your emotions, you allow room for states that cultivate creativity.

Focus

Meditation also helps with focus, which helps you to grow greater visions or ideas.[133] The more you practice directing your awareness into one single point and holding it there for a prolonged period of time without getting lost on a mental side track, the more you will soon be able to focus for longer periods. When learning to do this, you can employ a focal point such as a phrase, the image of a symbol in your

---

132 John J. Miller et al., "Three-Year Follow-Up and Clinical Implications of a Mindfulness Meditation-Based Stress Reduction Intervention in the Treatment of Anxiety Disorders," *General Hospital Psychiatry* 17, no. 3 (1995): 192–200, https://doi.org/10.1016/0163-8343(95)00025-M.

133 Davina Chan and Marjorie Woollacott, "Effects of Level of Meditation Experience on Attentional Focus: Is the Efficiency of Executive or Orientation Networks Improved?," *The Journal of Alternative and Complementary Medicine* 13, no. 6 (2007), https://doi.org/10.1089/acm.2007.7022.

mind's eye, or a point of sensation in your body, such as the feeling of your breath or your heartbeat.

When it comes to developing wisdom and especially intuitive knowledge, when you can focus and keep your attention on something, it imprints more deeply into your nervous system.[134] You begin to connect ideas across time through synchronicity. Wisdom is born from this kind of integrated understanding.

When we can keep our awareness on one train of thought without it getting broken off into other thoughts, we can more readily develop creative ideas and visions. Studies suggest that meditation can potentially enhance cognitive functions like memory and attention which are important for creativity. For example, meditation can increase activity in the hippocampus, an area of the brain associated with memory and imagination.[135]

Giving Form to Feeling

Meditation is useful when it comes to giving form to our emotions in order to bring subconscious wisdom to the surface. When you can sit with your feelings about something for long enough, they take form in symbol and language, but only when you can sit with them for sufficient time can you bring this wisdom to the surface. This is the process for finding order in the chaos of our emotions.

---

[134] Marvin M. Chun and Nicholas B. Turk-Browne, "Interactions between Attention and Memory," *Current Opinion in Neurobiology* 17, no. 2 (2007): 177–184, https://doi.org/10.1016/j.conb.2007.03.005.

[135] Anna Lardone et al., "Mindfulness Meditation Is Related to Long-Lasting Changes in Hippocampal Functional Topology during Resting State: A Magnetoencephalography Study," *Neural Plasticity* (2018), https://doi.org/10.1155/2018/5340717.

How the Imagination and Visualisation Can Be Used to Engage with Subconscious Wisdom

The ability to visualise concepts and engage your imagination is a very useful skill when it comes to working with the subconscious. When the subconscious speaks in symbols, it engages best with storytelling and visual cues, which explains why shamanic style meditations engage the imagination through storytelling methods and use characters and visual cues with deeply symbolic elements to trigger a response.

I find that when I am working with people on a one-on-one basis, I get to be more imaginative with the experience. For example, I remember I was guiding a lady who was struggling with a choice of where to live. I got her to imagine walking into different living spaces and making a quick choice while in a deep, still, state of meditation. That way she could decide based on how she felt intuitively rather than trying to calculate the likely result with her logical mind. She used her intuition to help her with her decision, exploring how she resonated with each outcome on a deeper level.

Another example is when I had someone who wanted to find clarity in his future career path and gain a clearer vision of a career in which he would find himself successful as an entrepreneur. Once I had guided him into a deep state of relaxation, I asked him to imagine stepping onto a stage. I painted a picture where he was being celebrated as the future version of himself that had achieved his goals. I then had a host on stage with him asking targeted questions about how he overcame his blocks and reached his success. Through this method, he was able to find answers and subconscious guidance to confidently follow to step into this version of himself.

How You Can Apply Symbolism to Engage Deeper Wisdom

To start with a simple example, if you imagine a warm, glowing red heart, you connect more to the feeling of love rather than just thinking of the word love.

In a guided meditation, when you are directed to think of two paths in front of you to walk down, symbolising the two lives you could live depending on which of two opposing options you choose, it's often easier to make a decision rather than just thinking of making a choice based on cool-headed logic.

I have seen again and again through personal experience and through guiding others that this method frequently works amazingly well. Many people say that they usually find themselves deliberating on decisions for ages, but using this technique makes it easy. Answers to questions that have been stuck for months just come to them without a second thought.

The technique I use is similar to the Jungian digging method or to shamanic journeying methods in meditation but is slightly more controlled. The Jungian digging method is a symbolic, psychological practice rooted in Carl Jung's theory of the unconscious; when utilising this method, one descends inward to interact with archetypes and uncover deeper truths for self-integration.

Shamanic journeying is a spiritual practice drawn from indigenous traditions which has similar properties to Jungian digging meditation. In the process of shamanic journeying, a person enters a trance state, often facilitated by drumming, to travel to non-ordinary realms and receive guidance from spirit guides, animals, or ancestors.

I practiced shamanic journeying for years with a shaman. I even spent an entire day meditating with this traditional shamanic method in a group. It's interesting to see what kinds of storylines, themes, or symbols come up. Sometimes the experiences can feel really random, but when you give yourself enough space and time to reflect, the reason behind your internal experience becomes more apparent.

How to Guide Yourself Through a Shamanic or Jungian Style Meditation

Sometimes when I have done these kinds of meditations without any specific intentions, questions, or structured symbolism in mind, I have broken through to profound and unexpected conclusions using this kind of dreamlike experience. At times, it feels like although I have control over my mental self walking through this journey in my mind's eye; the storyline or actual journey I end up on feels beyond my conscious control.

I have found myself in snowy landscapes and forests, by lakes and mountains, or in caves. I have met characters like speaking animals; one time I even met someone who told me to make a choice which surprised me. I made a decision then which surely shifted my life path in a way that felt most in alignment to me.

I think that one of the best demonstrations of experiencing symbolic wisdom in meditation comes from the following storyline, one that I experienced in my mind's eye through a method that I was taught. To give you a clearer sense of how symbolic wisdom unfolds in meditation, here's an extract from my personal meditation journal. This story, which emerged naturally during a deep state of stillness, illustrates how meditation can reveal profound insights through symbolic imagery:

I walked up the rough stone staircase, and it was cool. There was a slight breeze in the air, but it felt nice. At the top of the staircase was a door. It was made of aged, deep red wood, and the handle was vintage gold. I walked through, and there was snow as far as I could see.

I was barefoot, and I remember my toes going numb and the snow becoming ice under the pressure of my body. I saw something glimmering in the vast white landscape; it was a ring. I picked it up, put it on my finger mindlessly, and kept walking.

I heard a voice telling me to take it off, telling me that ownership is an empty illusion and that the true value comes in the moment, the experience. I listened and took the ring off. I looked at it again, and I saw a beauty in it that I had not seen before.

The loop of gold had a flat surface on the inside and a gentle even curve on the outside, and it was smooth to the touch. Four golden prongs grasped at a dark green emerald; the colours were so rich and the emerald was faceted so skilfully that I got lost trying to see through to the bottom of the gem.

I stayed here for a while admiring it. I put it down and moved on, still feeling more abundant than I'd initially felt when I put on the ring mindlessly. I kept walking, and the feeling faded; I went back to appreciate the ring for a second time, but I could not connect with it. It was just a ring.

• • •

I didn't think I had that kind of storyline in me, but I experienced it so naturally. I hadn't planned to have an experience like that exactly; it was like I was living the storyline, everything that happened was like I was experiencing it for the first time. At no point in this storyline did I know for sure what would happen next, it just happened.

This experience felt deeply meaningful for me this time in particular. It struck me as exactly what I needed to hear at the time—it always does. It demonstrates how the subconscious speaks in symbols and stories offering guidance beyond ordinary thought. The symbolism of the ring, its beauty, the invitation to release attachment, and the appreciation of the moment felt like a powerful lesson.

These experiences can be quite trippy depending on your state of mind, again in a way similar to psychedelic experiences. The psychedelic nature of these journeys isn't just about vivid visuals or sensations, but about uncovering deeper truths and aligning more closely with your authentic self.

The Meditation Structure

1. Begin by preparing a peaceful, dimly lit space where you can fully relax without interruptions. Turn off or silence your phone, and make sure you are wearing comfortable clothes. You could even light candles or incense to help create a space of calm.

2. To induce a state of hypnosis, either play a metronome at sixty beats per minute (mimicking the rhythm of your heartbeat) or play a track of a gentle drumbeat.

3. Lie comfortably on your back with your palms facing up, or sit with your back straight and your hands on your knees. Close your eyes and take a slow, deep breath in through your nose, then exhale softly through your mouth. Let each breath help you settle more deeply into the surface beneath you.

4. If any thoughts arise, keep dissolving them by bringing your awareness back to your breath; the longer you stay with a meditation practice, the easier this will be.

5. Imagine yourself standing in a dark space, taking time to bring awareness into your new body in your mind's eye. Imagine how the gravity of your body feels when you stand. Notice if there is a breeze in the air. Identify your various body parts and imagine how it feels to move them.
6. Imagine soft, muddy ground beneath you and a shovel in your hand, then dig into the ground. Keep digging down into the hole until you find yourself in a new world.
7. Observe this new world around you and feel free to explore it. Try walk into buildings or forests, or just do whatever you feel like doing. If you have come with the intention of answering a deep inner question, you can imagine meeting a guide and asking this guide to show you the answer. This being may either tell you the answer directly or take you on a journey.
8. Don't be afraid to explore whatever you may desire, but pay attention to what emerges in this state—what kind of situations or feelings arise.
9. When you feel ready to conclude your meditation session, slowly deepen your breath and begin to bring movement back to your fingers and toes. Stretch your arms and legs gently if you like. When you feel ready, open your eyes.
10. Write down your experience right away; like dream states, these experiences can be very easy to forget if they are not promptly recorded.

Chapter 8

Intuition in Terms of Pattern Recognition

Now, let's dig into intuition as a form of pattern recognition. Could this be a way of understanding intuitive phenomena that goes beyond what we have understood?

Intuition is understood by many to be a deep form of pattern recognition. The subconscious mind is capable of picking up on information that the conscious mind misses, including noticing patterns that don't even register on a conscious level.[136]

All the subtle information that lies in our field of awareness gets filtered through to the depths of our minds; our subconscious finds the patterns in this information and draws together synchronicities. These unconscious conclusions lie there in the depths of our minds as subconscious wisdom.

Many people think that pattern recognition in itself is enough to demystify intuitive phenomena. This belief holds that when we feel something to be true and can't put a label to why, it's because

---

[136] Miryam Naddaf, "How Your Brain Detects Patterns in the Everyday: Without Conscious Thought," *Nature*, September 25, 2024, https://www.nature.com/articles/d41586-024-03116-8.

we missed something obvious that our subconscious remembered. Let's say that someone told you their name and you completely forgot the conversation, but a few days later you met them again and had a "feeling" that their name is John, a feeling that turned out to be right. Someone might experience something like this and interpret it as psychic phenomena. This is an example of how the subconscious can hold onto information that goes beyond the conscious mind, and this information can be experienced as a feeling; but it's not always this simple.

The intelligence of subconscious pattern recognition reaches beyond simply recalling information in our surroundings that we have forgotten. The range that our general awareness and inner senses can reach and our ability to perceive the subtle determines the amount of material that the unconscious can distil into intuitive knowledge.

What if patterns exist in the universe that go beyond our comprehension? What if your level of consciousness or awareness is determined by your ability to perceive these patterns to different degrees?

Fractal universe theory suggests that everything exists in patterns and that life all follows a geometry, a concept on which I will expand soon.

Vibrational Sensitivity

If you have been into spirituality, it is likely you have come across the idea that intuitive phenomena or psychic phenomena is a kind of form of "vibrational sensitivity" that comes from a heightened degree of awareness.

Perhaps you have heard phrases like "trust your vibes" or "vibes don't lie." But what does this actually mean? Where do these ideas come from, and what is so special about vibration?

Hermetic traditions believe that the universe is vibrational—that everything is vibration. In *The Kybalion*, a Hermetic text, it states:[137]

"nothing rests, everything moves, everything vibrates"

Scientifically, we now understand this to be true in the physical world. Even matter is made up of vibrating particles. Vibration is all around us, carrying information that we can't see. Radio frequency waves are a great example. Although we can't deny their existence, we can't touch them, we can't see them, and we can't hear them—yet they carry information through frequency, including music, voices, and even entire data streams. Vibrations can carry information, and we decode them by recognising patterns within them. When you get a vibration wave up on a screen, you will see that it has a clear pattern.

---

[137] The Three Initiates, *The Kybalion: A Study of the Hermetic Philosophy of Ancient Egypt and Greece* (Yogi Publication Society, 1908).

Sand showing the pattern of a vibrating plate in cymatic studies

Vibration is what you find in the blurry lines of human perception. There is a vibrational spectrum that goes from what we can perceive into what goes beyond our awareness; In signal theory and neural dynamics, richer information is often carried in higher-frequency components or resonant interactions. Subtle patterns that are harder to perceive but encode more detail.[138] Sound vibration is a good example of this, but there are other subtle forces that exist, and so how this shows up isn't linear.

138 György Buzsáki and Xiao-Jing Wang, "Mechanisms of Gamma Oscillations," *Annual Review of Neuroscience* 35 (2012): 203–225, https://doi.org/10.1146/annurev-neuro-062111-150444.

Frequency in Neuroscience

In neuroscience, when it comes to our brainwave frequencies, our mind operates at different frequencies depending on our state of consciousness.[139]

For example:

Delta waves (0.5–4 Hz): deep sleep

Theta waves (4–8 Hz): meditation, creativity, dreams

Alpha waves (8–13 Hz): relaxation, alertness

Beta waves (13–30 Hz): focused thinking

Gamma waves (30–100+ Hz): heightened awareness, insight

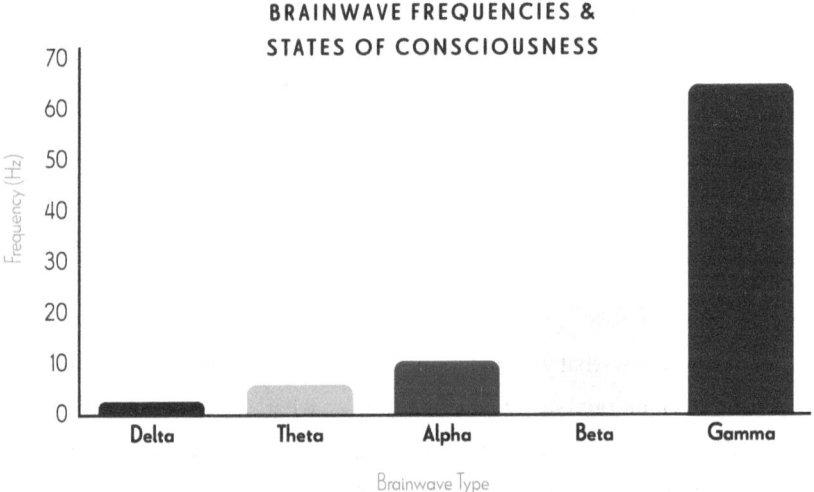

[139] Avgis Hadjipapas et al., "Editorial: Why the Exact Frequencies in Our Brains Matter: Perspectives from Electrophysiology and Brain Stimulation," *Frontiers in Systems Neuroscience* 16 (2023), https://doi.org/10.3389/fnsys.2022.1121438.

Gamma waves, which are the highest measurable brainwaves, are associated with states of expanded awareness and high-level information processing; but they're also the most difficult to detect and are often overlooked in standard EEG scans because their amplitude is lower, making them harder to pick up.[140,141] Studies have shown gamma activity increases during moments of deep insight, meditation, and mystical experiences.[142] Advanced meditators like Tibetan monks have shown strong gamma synchrony during deep states of compassion or non-dual awareness.[143]

Quantum Physics

Just as our brain operates with subtle frequencies that shape consciousness, modern physics reveals that at the foundation of reality, vibrations in quantum fields govern the behaviour of matter and energy. This suggests a fascinating parallel between how consciousness processes information and how the universe itself is structured. Quantum physics also demonstrates how more subtle vibrations contain more information.

Quantum physics, in essence, theorises that a particle is not a thing, but a dynamic state: a temporary form that emerges when a

---

140 "What to Know About Gamma Brain Waves," *WebMD*, October 1, 2025, https://www.webmd.com/brain/what-to-know-about-gamma-brain-waves.

141 Suresh Muthukumaraswamy, "High-Frequency Brain Activity and Muscle Artifacts in MEG/EEG: A Review and Recommendations," *Frontiers in Human Neuroscience* 7 (2013), https://doi.org/10.3389/fnhum.2013.00138.

142 Juergen Fell et al., "From Alpha to Gamma: Electrophysiological Correlates of Meditation-Related States of Consciousness," *Medical Hypotheses* 75, no. 2 (2010): 218–224, https://doi.org/10.1016/j.mehy.2010.02.025.

143 Xiaoli Guo et al., "Progressive Increase of High-Frequency EEG Oscillations during Meditation Is Associated with Its Trait Effects on Heart Rate and Proteomics: A Study on the Tibetan Buddhist," *Cerebral Cortex* 32, no. 18 (2022): 3865–3877, https://doi.org/10.1093/cercor/bhab453.

field is energized in a particular way. It's not that there's a particle in the field, but rather that the particle is the field vibrating.

These vibrational states vary in frequency, amplitude, and phase. Just as a musical instrument can play different notes when the player changes how its strings vibrate, various particles (and their associated forces) can similarly be understood as different vibrational "modes" of the underlying fabric of reality.

This means that at the deepest level, all of physical existence, including light, matter, and force, is composed of vibration structured into form through resonance and pattern.

Heisenberg's uncertainty principle, which states that the position and momentum of a particle cannot both be known precisely, speaks to the blurry and probabilistic nature of perception at quantum scales. Reality at this level is neither fixed nor sharply defined, but exists as a field of potential or even a soup of probability until it is observed or measured. This aligns almost eerily with ancient esoteric teachings that describe reality as fluid and shaped by subtle forces.

A property that is perhaps most profound in the context of vibration and subtle patterns is that these vibrational fields carry enormous amounts of information. The frequency of a vibration often correlates with its energy and information density. Higher frequency vibrations contain more complexity, but they're also more difficult to access or perceive, requiring increasingly sensitive instruments, just as how higher frequency brain states are harder to pick up on.

The ability to become sensitive or aware enough to come into a greater awareness of the subtle forces in our environment and recognise the patterns within them may be a gateway to not only understanding the deeper structure of reality itself, but also the ability to perceive information that reaches the extent of what we are capable of perceiving.

Pythagoras

The Greek philosopher Pythagoras believed that God was a number and held that this number was the fundamental principle of all reality. If all beings and things that exist were numbers, all would be patterns too, which again speaks to the idea of geometry.

Tesla

Nikola Tesla also had many interesting beliefs that spoke to the idea that the nature of the universe follows numbers and geometry. He saw the world in code and patterns. He was also particularly fascinated by vibration and adopted the idea that the nature of the universe itself was vibrational. He believed that understanding vibration was a fundamental key to understanding the nature of the universe. A quote often attributed to Tesla:

> "If you want to find the secrets of the universe, think in terms of energy, vibration and number."
> – Tesla

Tesla held the following views:

- Atoms vibrate at specific frequencies.
- Sound, light, and even thought are forms of energy traveling on waves.

- The earth itself has a resonant frequency (later called the "Schumann resonance," with the fundamental—the lowest frequency of a complex sound—at ~7.83 Hz).[144,145,146]

The Geometry of Comprehension

"What we call chaos is just patterns we have not recognised." – Chuck Palahniuk[147]

If everything in existence is vibrational, that would mean that everything has a pattern and that life itself has a rhythm.

Is there true chaos or are there only patterns that exist beyond our comprehension?

We see order and geometry in things that lesser forms of consciousness can only perceive as chaos.

We see the order in politics, but what is politics to a dog? What is science to a dog? A dog is bound to dog thoughts. It can't see existence beyond its own understanding. Do you think a dog really understands that we are smarter than it is? To a dog, there would be no reason for art, no reason for history, no reason for economy. They are not aware

---

144   "Nikola Tesla (1856–1943): Master of Resonance," The Physics of Resonance, Intuitor.com, http://intuitor.com/resonance/tesla.php.

145   Orrin E. Dunlap Jr., "An Inventor's Seasoned Ideas," *The New York Times*, April 8, 1934, https://teslauniverse.com/nikola-tesla/articles/tesla-sees-evidence-radio-and-light-are-sound.

146   "Nikola Tesla's Resonance Theories and the Schumann Resonance: An In-Depth Review," The Personal Site of Lalo Morales, https://www.laloadrianmorales.com/blog/nikola-teslas-resonance-theories-and-the-schumann-resonance-an-in-depth-review.

147   Chuck Palahniuk, *Survivor* (W. W. Norton, 1999).

that our language has meaning, let alone able to speak it, because it's chaos to them; and yet we see the order.

So, when there is a high probability of subjective levels of human consciousness and awareness, what is our equivalent of politics to a dog? We are the equivalent of magicians to dogs. Let's say your pet dog is injured and you take it to the vet: It won't understand what is happening. Perhaps in your dog's world, it would even have the qualities of a miracle.

This is something that really makes me wonder: If there were a higher form of consciousness than us, would we even see it? Would we recognise it, or are we too bound to our systems of thinking in the same way that a dog is? Our perception of what we think higher intelligence should look like is something that can only be met by our understanding. A truly higher form of consciousness would only be perceived as chaos by humans.

Metaphysically speaking, the systems of our minds are bound to various "geometries of understanding," which sounds quite abstract, but is something that is more easily recognised when we take all living things into account in the equation as well as how we view lesser and higher conscious life forms.

Simple bugs and plants are viewed as lesser forms of consciousness that can be fully comprehended by us to the point that we can almost exactly mathematically calculate their life cycles. They live to a simple geometry. Even in bugs, we can see through the geometric nature of what they create how their expressions also reflect this geometry: for example, honeycombs or spider webs.

Then we have animals such as cats and dogs that are more chaotic in nature than plants and bugs. They play around more and display heightened emotional complexity.

Still, though, they are not chaotic to us because we are more conscious. Where they see chaos, we see order. Would it not be ignorant to say that chaos to us is the only true chaos? I don't believe in true chaos. I believe chaos to be a subjective state that is a result of our inability to see the order in things.

Knowledge has dimensions, and it seems that our level of consciousness is determined by our ability to process and recognise patterns in different degrees of chaos.

Fractal Universe Theory

The idea that there is an intelligent geometry in the universe that reaches beyond our comprehension can be explained by fractal universe theory. This is an idea that I developed only to discover how deeply this way of thinking is reflected in the ideas of so many others.

Fractals are a kind of geometry. A fractal is a pattern that is self-similar on different scales. They can be very basic and simple, but no matter how much you zoom in, the pattern will still remain self-similar. Think of the pattern of a fern plant. A fern leaf's pattern is self-similar in the sense that the pattern of the leaf itself repeats into smaller similar leaves that make up the structure of the main leaf. That's fractal geometry: self-similarity on different scales.

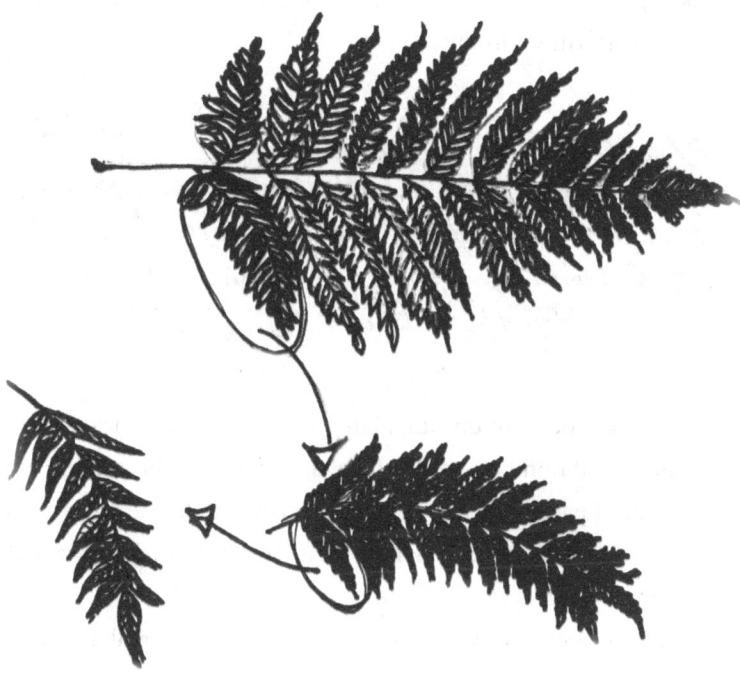

Fractals are not always so simple, however; in fact, most of the time they can reach complexities far beyond our comprehension. One of the most famous visual fractals is the Mandelbrot fractal.

It is generated by repetitively cycling a simple mathematical formula and examining the behaviour of points on the complex plane. It can only be comprehended when made visual. It is easier to grasp the nature of it if you can find a video zooming in or out of the fractal. This is the kind of geometry that is used to generate scenes in video games such as *Minecraft* or *Call of Duty*.[148]

Famous mathematician Benoit Mandelbrot, who came up with the Mandelbrot fractal, proposed that our universe is a fractal. What does this mean?

This would mean that life is a geometry set in motion by chaos, making life the flow of a complex equation working itself out and our life patterns set in time.

"Clouds are not spheres, mountains are not cones and bark is not smooth, nor does lightning travel in a straight line. My life seemed to be a series of events. Yet when I look back, I see a pattern." - Benoit Mandelbrot[149]

Fractals show up on our planet on different physical scales. Geometry and numbers are the language of our universe. There are small fractal patterns found in natural structures like feathers, fern leaves, curled shells, trees, and there are many more physically present in nature.

Fractal geometry can be scaled far beyond these small, physical, fractal patterns in nature into more complex, larger fractals, including the patterns of coastlines, river systems, rainforests, and even our cosmos. Our coastlines have fractal curve-like properties, which is

---

148   Adrian Cristea and Fotis Liarokapis, "Fractal Nature: Generating Realistic Terrains for Games," *IEEE Xplore* (2015), https://doi.org/10.1109/vs-games.2015.7295776.

149   "The Scope of Benoît Mandelbrot's Work and Its Influence," HistoryofScience.com., https://www.historyofscience.com/pdf/The%20Scope%20of%20Benoit%20Mandelbrot's%20Work%20and%20its%20Influence.pdf.

something known as the coastline paradox. River systems also have a fractal nature, as well as rain forests.

Terence McKenna did a talk about fractals, and he had heard of the coastline paradox.[150] He decided to test out the theory. He explained that he walked along a coastline and found a black pebble. He kept walking, and then he found what looked like the exact same pebble. This is when he then decided to test this idea; he traced his way back, counting his steps between the two points, and found that the total was seven hundred twenty-five steps. He took another seven hundred twenty-five steps in the other direction, and sure enough, he found a third pebble just like the other two.

McKenna said:[151]

> "What is implied if we say that there is a fractal description of rain forests, there's a fractal description of river systems, there is a fractal description of the coastlines? What that implies is that there must be a fractal in which those fractals are somehow subsets and that the planet itself is some kind of fractal object."
> —Terence McKenna

The Fractal Nature of the Cosmos

When we look into the cosmos with our high-powered telescopes, we see a universe that is far from uniform. It is a vast cosmic web of galaxies, each interconnecting in a complex pattern that spans the entire observable universe. These patterns reveal remarkable similarity to fractal structures. They follow a pattern that repeats at different scales.

---

150   Terence McKenna, "Terence McKenna on Fractals," posted on August 17, 2021, by We Plants Are Happy Plants, YouTube, 25 min., 27 sec., https://www.youtube.com/watch?v=qWKCsrwA1PY.

151   Terence McKenna, "Terence McKenna on Fractals," posted on August 17, 2021, by We Plants Are Happy Plants, YouTube, 25 min., 27 sec., https://www.youtube.com/watch?v=qWKCsrwA1PY.

The fractal nature of the cosmos can also be seen in the cosmic microwave background radiation—the afterglow of the Big Bang. The radiation shows slight variations in temperature, and these radiation temperatures appear to follow a fractal pattern: an endless dance of creation and destruction, of galaxies being born and dying, all following a fractal pattern.

These patterns even show up beyond physicality. The nature of language is fractal-like, and even the nature of our thoughts, including how we experience time in weeks, months, years. There is an undeniable rhythm to life that we live and follow. Did you know that we think around 95 percent of the same thoughts in one day that we thought the day before?[152] We live to a daily rhythm, a pattern.

We even experience weeks similarly. We collectively experience Mondays as the most tiresome and Wednesdays as "hump" days, and on Fridays, Saturdays, Sundays, we tend to let go a bit more. The rhythm of our daily routine fits into a larger rhythm of weeks, months, and even years. Collectively, how we experience the winter is different to the summer.

Fractal Phenomena in Psychedelic Experiences

I found it very interesting to notice that when I had reached my own conclusion about the fractal nature of the universe (which was, at the time, separate to my research trying to understand intuitive phenomena and DMT), a lot of the popular content I was finding on the internet was fractal-infused psychedelic art, including many

---

[152] Joe Dispenza, *Breaking the Habit of Being Yourself: How to Lose Your Mind and Create a New One* (Hay House, 2013).

articles about people claiming to see all kinds of fractal-like patterns and geometry during psychedelic trips.

Terence McKenna describes DMT experiences as exploding into "hyperdimensional spaces filled with fractal architecture" where reality unfolds in "impossible" geometries that are often self-similar and recursive.[153]

Why would people be seeing fractal geometry in altered and heightened states of consciousness?

It also amused me as an intuitive person that I was naturally drawn to the same topics as psychonauts. It surprised people with whom I was talking that I didn't take psychedelics, but rather arrived at these conclusions naturally, which I attribute to meditations.

Returning to the idea that DMT in the body could either be responsible for intuitive phenomena or highly involved in the psychology of intuition, it has been proven that pattern recognition significantly improves when a person is under the influence of psychedelics.[154]

In an interesting parallel, when it comes to the power of meditations, meditation has also been known to improve pattern recognition.[155] Some theorise that this is because meditation enhances attention, cognitive flexibility, and emotional regulation, all of which are crucial for identifying and understanding patterns. By training attention and awareness, meditation allows individuals to better observe their thoughts, emotions, and sensory perceptions, leading to

---

[153] Terence McKenna, *True Hallucinations: Being an Account of the Author's Extraordinary Adventures in the Devil's Paradise* (HarperOne, 1994).

[154] Shakila Meshkat et al., "Impact of Psilocybin on Cognitive Function: A Systematic Review," *Psychiatry and Clinical Neurosciences* 78, no. 12 (2024): 744–764, https://doi.org/10.1111/pcn.13741.

[155] Julia C. Basso et al., "Brief, Daily Meditation Enhances Attention, Memory, Mood, and Emotional Regulation in Non-Experienced Meditators," *Behavioral Brain Research* 356 (2019): 208–220, https://doi.org/10.1016/j.bbr.2018.08.023.

a deeper understanding of patterns in both internal experiences and external stimuli.[156]

As we bring our awareness deeper into the psyche, there's evidence to suggest that increased introspection can lead to a greater ability to recognise patterns, which can improve overall cognitive abilities and problem-solving. But if intuition and intuitive phenomena are a result of deep unconscious pattern recognition too, meditations are bound to improve our ability to manifest intuitive phenomena, which is what so many esoteric traditions have been saying for millennia.

The Fractal and Symbolic Nature of Wisdom

The fractal patterns observed everywhere in the universe from coastlines to cosmic webs suggest that intuition may involve recognising similar patterns in the subconscious. Building on the idea that psychedelic experiences reveal fractal-like geometries, wisdom itself appears to exhibit a fractal symbolic structure.

By "fractal-like," I mean patterns that repeat across scales from personal to cosmic; by "symbolic," I refer to archetypal forms that resonate with the subconscious as seen in meditation or dreams.

The following spiral wisdom example illustrates how intuition may decode universal patterns, applying insights from small experiences to broader contexts:

---

[156] Andrea Calderone et al., "Neurobiological Changes Induced by Mindfulness and Meditation: A Systematic Review," *Biomedicines* 12, no. 11 (2024): 2613, https://doi.org/10.3390/biomedicines12112613.

Spiral Wisdom

- **Personal Growth:** Personal growth follows a spiral, in which individuals revisit challenges with increasing wisdom and maturity, learning from past experiences to handle similar situations more effectively.

- **Social Systems and Communities:** Communities evolve by revisiting past issues and adapting old solutions to new contexts, building resilience and strength through each cycle.

- **The Environment:** Ecosystems regenerate through recurring cycles of life, death, and renewal, growing more complex and stable over time as they adapt to changing conditions.

- **Technology:** Technological advancement spirals forward by revisiting and refining old ideas, using new knowledge to create more advanced solutions.

- **History:** History evolves in a spiral, with societies learning from past mistakes and triumphs to build more sophisticated systems of governance and peace.

- **Cosmic and Evolutionary Scales:** The universe's growth follows a spiral, with stars and galaxies evolving. Each cycle of creation and destruction contributes to the cosmos's ongoing transformation.

As you can see, when you understand spiral wisdom as an essence, it unlocks many doors of understanding. When you comprehend one small thing, you can apply its symbolic value in many contexts.

Archetypal symbols such as these are deeper patterns that show up metaphysically. This isn't just the case for the spiral symbol but for many other shapes as well, which often show up as symbols with metaphysical properties in history.

This is something that illuminates the concept of meditating on certain symbols as a method of developing deeper wisdom. Certain geometries have particularly strong metaphysical properties; a lot of people would refer to this kind of archetypal geometry as sacred geometry, which often shows up in historic religious architecture too.

Something quite profound to take away from this is that the small things we do or come to understand can serve as keys to unlocking larger doors, even if we don't see them right away. To the subconscious, every action we take has a symbolic value.

When you understand one thing, often all of a sudden you have symbolically unlocked a whole new wave of clarity and understanding in multiple ways in your life. Everything is in a constant state of becoming, and each step, no matter how small, contributes to a larger process of growth and transformation.

Forms of Divination: Synchronicities in Understanding in Ancient Divination and the Principles of Fractal Universe Theory

Divination is something that was more popular in ancient civilisations but is still used today in many ways. I too like to use it sometimes in my own fashion. Divination methods are techniques used to supposedly give us a way to look into the unknown. They are used to make predictions or gain deeper insight into things beyond what can logically be known.

Patterns are everywhere; there is a geometry to everything, even if we can't always see all the patterns or comprehend it all. This inherent geometry does make us wonder about ancient forms of divination such as the I Ching, astrology, and numerology, which were all considered ancient forms of mathematics.

If patterns, geometry, and numbers can go beyond our comprehension, but we can perceive different levels of patterns in the universe depending on subjective levels of consciousness, that surely implies that psychic phenomena are possible. A sensitive person with strong pattern recognition can see order and gain information where someone less sensitive who has weaker pattern recognition ability perceives only chaos; a pattern might even fly under their radar completely. If awareness and pattern recognition are subjective factors that increase with intuition, there must be levels to how much information we can pick up. If the universe is truly fractal in nature, it not only expands our understanding of how far pattern recognition (and, by extension, intuition) can reach but also lends deeper credibility or insight into the thoughts behind these ancient divination systems. It suggests that what we've historically considered psychic knowledge may at least in part stem from deep subconscious pattern recognition and that ancient systems like the I Ching or astrology may reflect symbolic attempts to map or interface with this hidden order.

It would mean that there is an order in the chaos of chance, that there is some kind of order in the random card pulled from a tarot deck, in the rolling of dice, in the tea leaf residue at the bottom of a cup.

Does it mean anything to us, though?

What could the possibility of a truth beyond our comprehension possibly mean to us?

You can make of it what you like, but for me it affirms the importance of having a good relationship with the unknown: not fearing it, but embracing it, embracing the phases of chaos and uncertainty.

How could the ancients possibly know about fractal geometry, though? As I have said before, I believe that the ancients were particularly wise and in tune with their intuition and tapped into subconscious experience, which is where deep pattern recognition takes place. This would also explain the incredible, beautiful yet complex geometry found in so many places of ancient worship.

In Hermeticism and alchemy, the world view they describe affirms an understanding of the fractal-like nature of the universe. The most direct example of this is the alchemical concept of the microcosm and the macrocosm.

The Microcosm and Macrocosm

The microcosm and the macrocosm are concepts that are summarized by the famous Hermetic axiom "As above, so below."

as above, so below
as the universe, so the soul

In alchemy, the macrocosm is the great world: the vast universe, the cosmos, and divine order. This concept reflects planetary movements, celestial influences, and the alchemical transformations of nature.

The microcosm is the human being. Just as the universe undergoes cycles of change and transformation, so do the body, mind, and soul. In alchemy, the body's internal processes were seen as mirrors of cosmic alchemical transformations.

Ancient alchemists believed that the same forces governing the stars also shape human existence, and the existence of all living things, for that matter. Alchemical philosophy held that what is within us reflects in the cosmos and what is in the cosmos also reflects within us, which would reflect a fractal-like way of seeing the world.

I like this way of thinking because it empowers an infinity in our actions, in our thoughts. It makes every tiny thing cosmically significant.

Meditating on Symbols to Develop Deeper Wisdom

Now you understand how symbols carry psychologically deep wisdom. All of a sudden, the ancient ritual of meditating on symbols for different forms of wisdom seems less strange. Hypothetically, the more that you meditate and therefore impress a symbol with deep archetypal and metaphysical value onto your subconscious, the more that you are able to recognise the properties of this symbol showing up for you in your day-to-day.

If you focus on, say, a mandala that symbolises wholeness, or the Tree of Life, which represents growth and interconnectedness, you're essentially programming your subconscious with its archetypal essence. This "impression" works through repetition and giving the symbol your emotional attention, creating neural pathways that heighten your sensitivity to related themes.[157]

Psychologically, this aligns with concepts like priming (where exposure to a stimulus influences later perceptions) and confirmation bias (but in a positive, intentional way).

Metaphysically, it echoes ideas from Hermetic traditions or even quantum observer effects where focused intention shapes reality by drawing synchronicities into your orbit.

---

[157] Carl G. Jung, *The Collected Works of C. G. Jung, Volume 9 (Part I): The Archetypes and the Collective Unconscious*, ed. and trans. Gerhard Adler and R. F. C. Hull (Princeton University Press, 1969).

For instance, if you're meditating on the symbol of the phoenix (signifying rebirth from the ashes), you might start noticing resurrection motifs everywhere: a friend overcoming a setback, a plant reviving after neglect, or even a news story about renewal. It's not magic per se, but a heightened awareness that makes the world feel more alive and interconnected. The more you do it, the stronger the feedback loop becomes—recognition reinforces the symbol's power, deepening your wisdom and intuition.

How to Do a Symbol Point of Focus Meditation

1. Begin by preparing a peaceful, dimly lit space where you can fully relax without interruptions. Turn off or silence your phone, and make sure you are wearing comfortable clothes. You could even light candles or incense to help create a space of calm.

2. Play a relaxing background track such as nature sounds, a soft vibration harmony, or a long track of gentle music.

3. Sit with a straight back and your hands on your knees. For your focus, either keep a photo of an object with a symbolic value that you wish to invite into your life in front of you, or an object with symbolic value that you can hold in your hand.

4. Take a few moments to bring all of your awareness to the symbol until you have it suspended in your mind; imagine it in your mind's eye before closing your eyes.

5. Take a deep breath in through your nose, then exhale softly through your mouth. Let each breath help you settle more deeply into the surface beneath you and keep putting your energy into that visualisation.

6. If any thoughts arise, dissolve them by bringing your awareness back to your breath. The longer you continue with a meditation practice, the easier this will be.

7. Imagine yourself standing in a dark space; take time to bring awareness into your new body.

8. With each breath, imagine the properties of the symbol getting stronger. Whether the symbol brings, for example, a feeling of transformation or of release, whatever it might be, invite it into your mind's eye.

9. When you feel ready to conclude your practice, slowly deepen your breath and begin to bring movement back to your fingers and toes. Stretch your arms and legs gently if you like. When you feel ready, open your eyes.

Chapter 9

How Meditation Enhances Intuition

❖❖

The Relationship Between Meditation and Wisdom

What *is* wisdom? How do we become wise? Why is it that the great majority of wise philosophers have a meditation practice? **Let's take a look into the lifestyles of gurus and philosophers in the East and the West.**

In the East, there are many wise gurus, intelligent people with a rich understanding of the world and depth in their philosophies. People line up to ask them questions about their lives: how to overcome obstacles, how to see through to the light in times of darkness, or how to gain clarity on anything that they have been struggling with. Many gurus come to have substantial followings for their wisdom and teachings, and they all attribute their wisdom to one thing: meditation.

Many Eastern philosophers have advocated for meditation as a profound key to unlock this inner knowing and deeper levels of wisdom; this is what they became popular for. But this is not something that only shows up in the East.

Great Western philosophers also meditated, although many had other practices and methods of deep introspection that didn't look like sitting in meditation in the traditional sense.

Despite the fact that ancient Greece had no formal meditation tradition, Socrates, who is known as the father of Western philosophy, used to engage in a few practices that essentially were their own forms of meditation. For example:

Socrates used to suddenly freeze for hours in thought. This is something that is explored in Plato's *Symposium*, which even describes him once standing motionless from dawn until noon. In the year 432 BCE, at a military camp during the Siege of Potidaea, his fellow warriors gathered around him in awe; some even slept nearby in order to observe him. Despite the commotion, Socrates remained completely absorbed, as if in a transcendent state.

There are a few ways that this parallels a traditional meditation practice:

Socrates' trance mirrors advanced yogic *samādhi* or the Zen practice of *zazen*, during which mental chatter ceases and awareness merges with "pure being." Plato called this *theoria* (meaning "contemplation of divine truth"). Despite freezing temperatures, Socrates felt no discomfort—a phenomenon also documented in Himalayan yogis who meditate barefoot in snow. Also, upon "returning," Socrates prayed calmly and behaved normally, suggesting integrated insight like that of a monk concluding a deep meditation.

Socrates was not the only Western philosopher to intuitively take up a form of meditation or conscious mindfulness.

Arthur Schopenhauer, often called "the philosopher of the will," advocated for something that he called "will-less perception," which is essentially just a state of pure observation akin to mindfulness.

Friedrich Nietzsche, one of the most well-known Western philosophers, used to regularly do a walking meditation of sorts. He composed his philosophy while hiking for eight or more hours daily. He declared, "All truly great thoughts are conceived while walking."[158] A walking meditation practice is one of the lesser-known forms of meditation, but it's one of my favourite meditations to do.

Leonardo da Vinci also liked to exercise shifting his point of awareness as a practice. He would completely absorb himself in objects that others might see as mundane, a form of contemplation which can be described as a form of open monitoring meditation. While da Vinci wasn't strictly a philosopher in the traditional sense, his genius bridged art, science, and a deeply contemplative approach to existence that ultimately reshaped society.

He would fix his gaze on walls stained with dampness or on random stone patterns for hours, allowing his mind to project creative visions, a practice which is also similar to modern image streaming, *kasina* meditation, or even my favourite shamanic and Jungian active imagination meditations.

Image streaming is a more active meditation practice; it's a visualisation technique that was developed by Win Wenger, PhD, in the 1970s to enhance cognitive abilities. It requires a meditative state of mind that is relaxed but focused.

The practice of image streaming involves allowing spontaneous mental images to arise and describing them aloud or in writing in vivid, sensory detail, ideally to another person or a recording

---

[158] Friedrich Nietzsche, "Why I Am So Clever," in *Ecce Homo: How One Becomes What One Is*, trans. R. J. Hollingdale (Insel-Verlag, 1908).

device. The process aims to strengthen the connection between the conscious and subconscious mind, unlocking deeper insights and creative potential. The idea is that by verbalizing these images in real time, you engage both hemispheres of the brain, fostering neural integration. It's akin to a meditative practice but emphasizes active verbalization over silent contemplation.

This way of shifting your perception to connect to things differently reminds me of one of my favourite quotes from the poetry of the visionary William Blake:[159]

> "To see a world in a grain of sand,
> and a heaven in a wild flower,
> Hold infinity in the palm of your hand,
> and eternity in an hour"
> – William Blake

This expresses the idea that as long as you can root your awareness fully into something rather than experiencing it passively, it can become an experience of far greater significance.

When you learn how to be present and focus well, your entire life becomes an opportunity to experience richly, with depth and meaning. When you really get to this stage in a meditation practice, the way that you move through life in general can change drastically. What you value and your relationship with materialism will naturally change when you can truly see how the key is in your perception.

---

[159] William Blake, "Auguries of Innocence," in *The Complete Poetry and Prose of William Blake*, ed. David V. Erdman (Anchor, 1988).

Wisdom as a Form of Intuitive Intelligence and the Relationship Between Meditation and Metaphysics

There is an undeniable relationship between meditation and metaphysics.

Metaphysics is a branch of philosophy that deals with things not grounded in materialism or strictly logical understanding, including concepts such as consciousness, love, symbolism, and will. Osho's teachings on consciousness and Socrates' *theoria* reflect metaphysical inquiry enabled by meditative states. All material science is derived from metaphysics. Often new ideas, before they are brought into material understanding, are first metaphysical concepts. It is this ability to think in a metaphysical manner that determines the creative and innovative ability required for scientific breakthrough.

Meditation is closely associated with metaphysics. The process of meditating opens the mind up, allowing the meditator to explore bigger ideas that aren't necessarily rooted in material laws. With a meditation practice, you are able to think more creatively and can break down your ego in a way that helps you to view things through a lens that isn't blinded by certainty. Meditation teaches the ability to detach from ideas and view things from different angles—to warp your perspective, if you will.

I don't want people to be put off by the big, complicated ideas that people project onto meditation—even my own, if you can't understand them. That is the nature of metaphysical teachings: Not everyone can understand certain things. Some things you can only connect to intuitively, and that mystery is their essence. Some say that makes certain metaphysical ideas special or secret. People like to keep them occult (meaning "hidden"), and I get it, but what good are metaphysical ideas if you can't work to ground them into physical reality? Without Tesla's ability to ground metaphysics into reality, modern technology including remotes, AC, and radios would simply be mystical "occult" ideas floating around the aether. We wouldn't have the working logistics to ground them into reality, and perhaps only an intuitive few would connect to the essence of their possibility.

Metaphysics is where all the mysteries and all the possibilities lie. It's the blurry lines between what is and what isn't possible. In its essence, I suppose that is quite mystical, but the benefits of being able to think from a more metaphysical perspective are undeniably profound.

Intuitive Wisdom vs. Logic

I view wisdom as a more intuitive intelligence than logic; wisdom is developed and grows richer with experience, whereas logic falls more on the surface. Plain cold logic is linear, whereas wisdom seems to be more of a felt sense of what is true or what is right. It is something that is felt before it is calculated, like a deep sense of synchronicity that guides us.

I have found that this deeply felt synchronicity connected to the essence of wisdom can be explained by the mysterious symbolic nature of the depths of our mind, which also gives us insights into how certain types of meditations work.

There is an undeniable relationship between wisdom and meditation. With a meditation practice, you can unlock your own inner wisdom, live life with a deeper layer of understanding and awareness and clarity, build your own philosophy, and find your own truth and meaning.

So many amazing philosophers and gurus have shared their wisdom, answering questions about all kinds of things and preaching meditation, all while many people take a surface approach and only come to ask for wisdom when they themselves have the power to look within to find the answers. Everyone has an inner guru—an inner voice waiting to be heard.

It's not always easy to start a meditation practice from scratch. Of course, I had an advantage having started so young. Many people say that they can't manage it; they say that their thoughts are too loud and they can't focus, but that is why meditation is a practice. It takes practice, dedication, and building up mental resistance to learn to be still. You must sacrifice some of your time to being uncomfortable before you are able to reap the incredible benefits of a meditation practice.

There is this false stereotype about meditation that is widely held particularly in the West: Because meditation is seen as such a symbol of relaxation and bliss, many people think that it should be bliss right away, and so they get stressed at the actual point when they start to meditate and all the uncomfortable thoughts that they have been trying to keep buried come to the surface.

Meditation is about becoming familiar with the mind, working with it, and learning to let go of thoughts that don't serve you. It is also about being able to hold your awareness on things that do serve you and on what you choose while acquiring the ability to let away thoughts that come to the surface. You yourself have the keys to the kingdom. You can begin to get into profoundly impactful meditations and techniques, although learning to focus and let go would already create profound enough change as it is.

Your brain is a muscle (figuratively speaking). Your thoughts are simply patterns following neural pathways that become stronger the more that you think those thoughts and weaker the more that you let them slip away.[160] Learning how to direct your awareness and apply your mind to your deeper intentions and will gives you freedom.

---

160 Ami Citri and Robert C. Malenka, "Synaptic Plasticity: Multiple Forms, Functions, and Mechanisms," *Neuropsychopharmacology Reviews* 33 (2008): 18–41, https://doi.org/10.1038/sj.npp.1301559.

Opening up new pathways of thought opens up paths and possibilities for you in your physical reality. Meditation gives you the ability to create space and focus deeper attention to open up mental doors, and doing this helps you achieve whatever outcome you desire, in the process emotionally conditioning yourself to connect to these possibilities more easily.

How Meditation Helps Us to Alter Our Perception

Emotions are lenses to our perception. Meditation gives us more control of our emotions and therefore clarifies our vision and our ability to utilise heightened states to reach desired outcomes. Your mind is the central point from which everything else comes into focus. Our emotions tint our vision, and when we find stillness and come into a state of presence or neutrality, we see things with the most clarity.

When you are in a bad mood, you are more likely to notice the negative things in your day that affirm how you already feel, and you will struggle to connect to the more positive things although they are still there.[161] You are more likely to notice the rubbish on the floor, your insecurities, where your blocks are, and the negative things about the relationships in your life.

In a bad mood, you aren't able to notice the positive things as easily; they are filtered out. A child laughing would be more likely to irritate you than bring you joy; when your friend texts with thoughtful intentions, you may appreciate it, but it might be harder to connect to. And the beauty in nature? It becomes white noise, meaningless.

---

[161] Aleksandr T. Karnick et al., "Negative Mood and Optimism Bias: An Experimental Investigation of Sadness and Belief Updating," *Journal of Behavior Therapy and Experimental Psychiatry* 82 (2024): 101910, https://doi.org/10.1016/j.jbtep.2023.101910.

This is why when you identify with a belief or a state of mind, it's harder to get out of that way of seeing the world because we condition ourselves to see the world through that lens. We blind ourselves to opposing information, falling into unconscious confirmation bias based on our emotional state.

You could live the exact same day, with the exact same experiences, in a different mood. You might pass the same people on the street and have the same set of tasks before you, but your experience will be entirely different. You will notice different things and reach different conclusions, and these conclusions become building blocks of our understanding.

As long as our awareness is fogged by emotion, we don't see the full picture; but our emotions make up who we are. Our identity is like an emotional signature, so to see things in absolute clarity all the time is unrealistic. It's good to feel, but it's also good to be aware of how our emotions may blind us. We should move through phases of feeling knowing that the nature of the reality that we experience is only a fragment of the full picture.

The more still you become, the more you learn how to move through your emotions, find your centre, and settle into neutrality, as well as how to see things clearly, connect to your intuition, and find answers on how to move past blockages. You will also develop more of a sense of control when moving through emotional states. Learning to shift your emotional states more to your will is something that is utilised in manifestation practices. When you are emotionally connected to something or in alignment emotionally with the version of yourself that already has the thing that you desire, you can physically see more paths, possibilities, and opportunities relating to your goals, while unhelpful ways of thinking or observations become less natural, making your goals more attainable. Our emotions are more powerful to our perception than many people realise. Meditation helps regulate emotions by engaging brain networks that manage emotional processing, reducing reactivity.[162]

The prefrontal cortex (PFC), which is responsible for decision-making and emotional regulation, is activated during meditation.[163] Studies show mindfulness meditation increases PFC grey matter density, enhancing control over impulsive emotional reactions.[164] A stronger prefrontal cortex supports discernment, which comes with mental clarity and self-reflection.

How Meditation Improves Focus and Memory as a Gateway to Higher Cognition

I went on a week-long silent Buddhist meditation retreat where we meditated five hours a day and were instructed not to speak or use our cell phones in order to foster deep introspection. To my surprise, we only did one meditation method again and again. This meditation was the simplest meditation, but its benefits were quite profound.

Single-Point Meditation

Single-point meditation is one of the best meditations for beginners. We would just focus on our breath the entire time—that's it. The idea seemed to be that the longer you are able to hold an object in your

---

[162] Simón Guendelman et al., "Mindfulness and Emotion Regulation: Insights from Neurobiological, Psychological, and Clinical Studies," *Frontiers in Psychology* 8 (2017), https://doi.org/10.3389/fpsyg.2017.00220.

[163] Singh Deepeshwar et al., "Hemodynamic Responses on Prefrontal Cortex Related to Meditation and Attentional Task," *Frontiers in Systems Neuroscience* 8 (2015), https://doi.org/10.3389/fnsys.2014.00252.

[164] Nicole Last et al., "The Effects of Meditation on Grey Matter Atrophy and Neurodegeneration: A Systematic Review," *Journal of Alzheimer's Disease* 56, no. 1 (2016): 275–286, https://doi.org/10.3233/jad-160899.

awareness without your mind drifting off or becoming distracted, the more you are able to focus on your day-to-day and the better your memory will ultimately function. Focus is the gateway to all higher cognition. If you can't pay attention, you can't think clearly. If you don't have the ability to focus to apply yourself to the activity you choose with your will, are you really free? Or are you just living unconsciously, chained to habits that don't really align with who you want to be and what you wish to achieve deep down? Your ability to act on your will takes focus and mental discipline, especially when what is needed to implement your decisions is outside your comfort zone.

Also, your ability to grow ideas is dependent on your ability to root your focus into the concept you are working with. Your ability to create and build is dependent on your ability to root your awareness in something, no matter what it is.

Weak focus + weak awareness = weak work.

As the Buddhists have been saying for thousands of years, there is indeed a science to the incredible benefits of even the simplest meditation. A 2013 study found that a two-week mindfulness training course enhanced working memory capacity and reduced mind-wandering, with participants showing improved performance on working memory assessment tasks such as the operation span task.[165] Similarly, a 2019 study demonstrated that eight weeks of brief daily meditation improved working memory and recognition memory in non-experienced meditators.[166]

This simple breathwork process is handy for beginners because the breath is something active, and so it's easier to root your awareness in

---

[165] Michael D. Mrazek et al., "Mindfulness Training Improves Working Memory Capacity and GRE Performance While Reducing Mind Wandering," *Psychological Science* 24, no. 5 (2013): 776–781, https://doi.org/10.1177/0956797612459659.

[166] Julia C. Basso et al., "Brief, Daily Meditation Enhances Attention, Memory, Mood, and Emotional Regulation in Non-Experienced Meditators," *Behavioral Brain Research* 356 (2019): 208–220, https://doi.org/10.1016/j.bbr.2018.08.023.

your breath. It's also important to practice being able to get to states of stillness first before engaging the imagination for insight.

THE MEDITATION

1. Begin by preparing a peaceful space where you can fully relax without interruptions. Turn off or silence your phone, and wear soft, loose clothing.

2. Find a comfortable position. You can either sit crossed legged or on a chair with your feet on the ground and your hands on your knees or on your back. Close your eyes and take a slow, deep breath in through your nose, then exhale softly through your mouth. Let each breath help you settle more deeply into the surface beneath you.

3. Bring all of your focus onto one single point. You can focus on a meaningful symbol in your mind's eye, a phrase, or a body part such as your heart space. I find that for beginners, the easiest point of focus is the breath.

4. When you find yourself getting distracted, gently come to an awareness of this train of thought and then shift your awareness back to your point of focus.

5. When you feel ready to conclude your practice, slowly deepen your breath and begin to bring movement back to your fingers and toes. When you feel ready, open your eyes.

How You Know You Are Connecting to Intuitive Information vs. Passing Thoughts

One of the most common and valid questions that people ask in regard to communicating to their subconscious for intuitive insight is: "How do I know that this is an intuitive insight and not something based on assumptions of the past?" Some people have intrusive thoughts or assumptions backed by anxiety, but there is a notable difference in how these types of thoughts are experienced.

Intuitive insight comes from a profound place; it is experienced very deeply and feels unshakable. It feels like a moment of clarity that emerges from a place of stillness. It's very different from the kind of intrusive thoughts that happen in moments of anxiety or elevated states. If you are feeling anxious or manic, you can't connect to your intuition very well at all. This is why meditation is so important for fostering your intuition.

Divination Methods

Traditionally, divination methods are used to connect to "information that goes beyond," and they are often seen in spiritual and mystic traditions as a bridge between realms.

Divination techniques can make use of things like:

- Crystal balls
- Astrology
- Numerology
- Tarot and oracle cards
- Pendulums

I don't think that these methods of divination are all purely superstitions; I believe there could be some truth to them that we do not yet fully understand. As I mentioned previously, it's already interesting how many of these divination methods utilise forms of mathematical calculation, which makes sense if you are open to the concept that our universe has fractal characteristics.

Let's go into more detail on how some of these methods are very useful tools to communicate with your subconscious mind and connect to your intuition, specifically the pendulum and crystal ball scrying method. Both of these methods are traditionally performed in a state of stillness that encourages an almost hypnotic state.

Crystal Ball Scrying Meditation

Returning to the image touched on earlier of the wise old woman gazing into the crystal ball in a still state of meditation, let's dig into the topic of crystal ball scrying so you can decide if this divination method is purely superstitious or if it can actually be a useful form of meditation to help you find clarity.

I was kindly gifted a rare occult book from the 1920s

called "crystal gazing" by Frater Achad, who was a Canadian occultist and ceremonial magician.

In the book, Achad speaks of crystal gazing as a discipline that serves as a bridge to achieving clear spiritual vision. He says that gazing into a crystal sphere initiates visions through focus on what he terms "the Lesser Crystalline Sphere." He explains that these visions, which he says are symbolic, have the ability to give insight into the past, present, and future but are unpredictable and depend heavily on the gazer's inner state.

The smooth, reflective surface of the crystal ball allows the gazer to project internal images or symbols onto it, and the act of gazing into a clear or slightly cloudy sphere can induce a state similar to a meditative trance.

In a meditative state, the crystal becomes a mirror into the depths of the psyche, a bit like how da Vinci used mundane objects for scrying; yet there also seems to be some sort of belief that the crystal sphere has some sort of significance that helps us to look deeper within ourselves. I believe it's more symbolic than anything, but as I have previously described, I believe that symbolism is a powerful tool to communicate with the subconscious.

The spherical shape of a crystal ball is symbolically associated with completeness and infinity, reflecting the idea of a unified consciousness or the universe's interconnectedness aligning with concepts like the "fractal nature of the universe" as previously mentioned. It also somewhat mirrors my model of the psyche as well, the one with the concentric layers.

The crystal sphere also acts as a single-point focus, similar to the breath in the single-point meditation described earlier in this chapter. By gazing into the sphere, the mind enters a meditative state; mental chatter is quieted and a hypnotic or trance-like state conducive to intuitive insights is fostered.

How Would You Perform a Crystal Gazing Session?

1. Make sure that you are in a place where you know you won't be interrupted. Set your phone on silent or put it in another room.

2. Making sure the room is dimly lit, set up your crystal ball with a candle lit behind it. Dim lighting reduces distractions, and the candle enhances the reflective quality of the sphere, making it more hypnotic.

3. Give yourself some time for journaling beforehand to get clear on the question or area on which you would like to find clarity.

4. Sitting in front of the crystal ball, meditate for ten minutes, focusing on your breath and the sensations of your body, I would even recommend the kundalini style breathwork process described in Chapter 4 to enhance the imagination.

5. When you are ready to come out of the meditation, gently gaze at the crystal ball while still in the meditative state. Do your best not to initiate any further thought patterns other than the question in the back of your mind. Loosening your grip on the question, explore what emerges for however long you feel is right or until you are able to reach a conclusion and explore any symbolism or unexpected messages that come up.

6. When you are finished with the crystal ball meditation, write down your conclusions since they can be easy to forget once you are no longer in the meditative state.

Pro Tip: Do this practice on an empty stomach to increase your mental activity, or consider drinking a mugwort tea blend beforehand to further enhance your imagination.

Pendulum Meditation

A pendulum is best described as an amulet strung on a single chain drawing down to a point; the amulet is often made from crystal, wood, or metal. This is a form of divination that gives a yes or no response to each of your questions as you hold it still and observe how it swings.

Pendulums have been used across cultures for centuries for both practical and mystical purposes. Their history spans scientific, spiritual, and divinatory applications. One of the earliest recorded uses of pendulums comes from ancient China, where they were employed in divination practices. Chinese texts describe "divining rods" and pendulum-like devices used to locate water or minerals, which is a practice that in English is called dowsing. These methods were believed to tap into unseen energies or intuitive knowledge. Ancient Egyptians also used pendulums in a similar way. Priests and seers employed them in rituals to commune with spiritual forces, viewing their movements as messages from the divine.

Seers were people in ancient Egypt, often priests or priestesses, who were believed to possess the ability to access divine or hidden knowledge through visionary and intuitive practices. They were known as *rekh khet* ("those who know things").

The pendulum is actually a fantastic way to communicate with your subconscious because the subtle movements that are made are often subconsciously influenced even if you are consciously trying not to move your hand.

Pendulum Meditation

1. First, as with the crystal ball meditation, make sure you are in a place where you are not going to be disturbed; set your phone on silent, and keep the lights dim.

2. Establish the question on which you would like more clarity, and then establish which way the pendulum will swing when you want a "yes" answer or a "no" answer. Possibilities include the pendulum moving front and back, side to side, or in a circle.

3. Meditate for ten minutes, focusing on your breath and grounding into the feeling of presence.

4. Hold your pendulum at the top of the chain, letting it come to the centre before asking your question either out loud or in your mind's eye; take a little time while patiently waiting for a response.

5. You can ask a couple of questions here before ending the divination session.

Conclusion

Magic Exists

I have spent my entire life trying to rationalise the impossible, working to make sense of these strange intuitive experiences that I couldn't shake, experiences that made me feel like an alien.

I wanted to find a science for these intuitive phenomena and demystify these practices so that more people who had never had such experiences could open to them. I found something good enough for me to understand it in my own way. It feels like my feet are on the ground. I hope I have also helped you to see the possibilities that lie within yourself—to know that there is something deep within you that you can trust, something that will guide you even when you can't see a way.

But I now see that magic exists too. There is an ever-present mystery in that strange metaphysical grey zone between what we think we know to be true and what is possible. That grey zone is where the magic is, in the place right between chaos and order. It is the field from which all new knowledge is birthed, the place we go at three to four in the morning, in the depths of meditation and in birth and death.

That mystery, that magic lies at the core of your being. It's in the very essence of your consciousness: a knowing.

It's there for you whenever you are ready to slow down enough to meet it.

References

Allen, Annette E. "Circadian Rhythms in the Blind." *Current Opinion in Behavioral Sciences* 30 (2019): 73–79. https://doi.org/10.1016/j.cobeha.2019.06.003.

Anthony, J. E. C., A. Winstock, J. A. Ferris, and D. J. Nutt. "Improved Colour Blindness Symptoms Associated with Recreational Psychedelic Use: Results from the Global Drug Survey 2017." *Drug Science, Policy and Law* 6 (2020). https://doi.org/10.1177/2050324520942345.

Ardura, Julio, Regina Gutierrez, Jesus Andres, Teresa Agapito. "Emergence and Evolution of the Circadian Rhythm of Melatonin in Children." *Hormone Research in Paediatrics* 59, no. 2 (2003): 66–72. https://doi.org/10.1159/000068571.

Arendt, Josephine, and Anna Aulinas. "Physiology of the Pineal Gland and Melatonin." In *Endotext*, edited by K. R. Feingold, S. F. Ahmed, B. Anawalt, et al. MDText.com, Inc., 2000–. Updated October 30, 2022. https://www.ncbi.nlm.nih.gov/books/NBK550972.

Aristotle. *On the Soul (De Anima)*. Translated by J. A. Smith and W. D. Ross. Clarendon Press, 1908.

Bagnol, Lulu, Jeff Alexander, Helen Ewing, and Dorus Chu. "Indigos in Hawai'i: A Phenomenological Study of the Experience of Growing

Up with Spiritual Intelligence." *Pacific Health Dialog* 17, no. 1 (2011): 83–98. https://pubmed.ncbi.nlm.nih.gov/23008973.

Bakewell, Cathy, and Vincent-Wayne Mitchell. "Male Versus Female Consumer Decision Making Styles." *Journal of Business Research* 59, no. 12 (2006): 1297–1300. https://doi.org/10.1016/j.jbusres.2006.09.008.

Bargh, John A., and Tanya L. Chartrand. "The Unbearable Automaticity of Being." *American Psychologist* 54, no. 7 (1999): 462–479. https://doi.org/10.1037/0003-066X.54.7.462.

Barker, Steven A., Ethan H. McIlhenny, and Rick Strassman. "A Critical Review of Reports of Endogenous Psychedelic N, N-dimethyltryptamines in Humans: 1955–2010." *Drug Testing and Analysis* 4, no. 7–8 (2012): 617–635. https://doi.org/10.1002/dta.422.

Barker, Steven A. "N, N-Dimethyltryptamine (DMT), an Endogenous Hallucinogen: Past, Present, and Future Research to Determine Its Role and Function." *Frontiers in Neuroscience* 12 (2018). https://doi.org/10.3389/fnins.2018.00536.

Baron-Cohen, Simon. "Autism: The Empathizing-Systemizing (E-S) Theory." *The Year in Cognitive Neuroscience 2009* 1156, no. 1 (2009): 68–80. https://doi.org/10.1111/j.1749-6632.2009.04467.x.

Basso, Julia C., Alexandra McHale, Victoria Ende, Douglas J. Oberlin, and Wendy A. Suzuki. "Brief, Daily Meditation Enhances Attention, Memory, Mood, and Emotional Regulation in Non-Experienced Meditators." *Behavioral Brain Research* 356 (2019): 208–220. https://doi.org/10.1016/j.bbr.2018.08.023.

Bauer, Barbara E. "5-MeO-DMT, Toad Secretions, and the Entourage Effect." *Psychedelic Science Review*, May 16, 2019. https://psychedelicreview.com/5-meo-dmt-toad-venom-and-the-entourage-effect.

Berkovich-Ohana, Aviva, Meytal Wilf, Roni Kahana, Amos Arieli, and Rafael Malach. "Repetitive Speech Elicits Widespread Deactivation in the Human Cortex: The 'Mantra' Effect?" *Brain and Behavior* 5, no. 7 (2015): e00346. https://doi.org/10.1002/brb3.346.

Bharti, V. "Boron as an Antidote to Fluoride Toxicity." *Epidemiology* 18, no. 5 (2007): S109–S110. https://doi.org/10.1097/01.ede.0000288441.02944.26.

Blake, William. "Auguries of Innocence." In *The Complete Poetry and Prose of William Blake*, edited by David V. Erdman. Anchor, 1988.

Borjigin, Jimo, U. Lee, T. Liu, et al. "Surge of Neurophysiological Coherence and Connectivity in the Dying Brain." *Proceedings of the National Academy of Sciences* 110, no. 35 (2013): 14432–14437. https://doi.org/10.1073/pnas.1308285110.

Brebner, John. "Gender and Emotions." *Personality and Individual Differences* 34, no. 3 (2003): 387–394. https://doi.org/10.1016/S0191-8869(02)00059-4.

Bryant, Keaki. "Unveiling the Mystery of Meditation's Geometric Visions." ShunSpirit, September 27, 2024. https://shunspirit.com/article/why-do-i-see-geometric-shapes-when-i-meditate.

Buzsáki, György, and Xiao-Jing Wang. "Mechanisms of Gamma Oscillations." *Annual Review of Neuroscience* 35 (2012): 203–225. https://doi.org/10.1146/annurev-neuro-062111-150444.

Calderone, Andrea, Desirée Latella, Federica Impellizzeri, et al. "Neurobiological Changes Induced by Mindfulness and Meditation: A Systematic Review." *Biomedicines* 12, no. 11 (2024): 2613. https://doi.org/10.3390/biomedicines12112613.

Carhart-Harris, Robin L., and K. J. Friston. "REBUS and the Anarchic Brain: Toward a Unified Model of the Brain Action of Psychedelics." *Pharmacological Reviews* 71, no. 3 (2019): 316–344. https://doi.org/10.1124/pr.118.017160.

Carhart-Harris, Robin L., Robert Leech, Peter J. Hellyer, et al. "The Entropic Brain: A Theory of Conscious States Informed by Neuroimaging Research with Psychedelic Drugs." *Frontiers in Human Neuroscience* 8 (2014). https://doi.org/10.3389/fnhum.2014.00020.

Carskadon, Mary A., and William C. Dement. "Normal Human Sleep: An Overview." In *Principles and Practice of Sleep Medicine*, 5th ed. Saunders, 2011.

Central Intelligence Agency. *Analysis and Assessment of Gateway Process*. Wayne M. McDonnell. CIA-RDP96-00788R001700210016-5. Fort Meade, MD: US Army Operational Group, 1983. Online PDF, https://www.cia.gov/readingroom/docs/CIA-RDP96-00788R001700210016-5.pdf.

Chan, Davina, and Marjorie Woollacott. "Effects of Level of Meditation Experience on Attentional Focus: Is the Efficiency of Executive or Orientation Networks Improved?." *The Journal of Alternative and Complementary Medicine* 13, no. 6 (2007). https://doi.org/10.1089/acm.2007.7022.

Chu, Brianna, et al. *Physiology, Stress Reaction*. StatPearls Publishing, 2025.

Chun, Marvin M., and Nicholas B. Turk-Browne. "Interactions between Attention and Memory." *Current Opinion in Neurobiology* 17, no. 2 (2007): 177–184. https://doi.org/10.1016/j.conb.2007.03.005.

Citri, Ami, and Robert C. Malenka. "Synaptic Plasticity: Multiple Forms, Functions, and Mechanisms." *Neuropsychopharmacology Reviews* 33 (2008): 18–41. https://doi.org/10.1038/sj.npp.1301559.

"Color Vision Problems Become More Common with Age, Study Shows." *ScienceDaily*, February 24, 2014. https://www.sciencedaily.com/releases/2014/02/140220102614.htm.

Confer, Joshua A., Hanna Schleihauf, and Jan M. Engelmann. "Children and Adults' Intuitions of What People Can Believe." *Child Development* 95, no. 2 (2024): 447–461. https://doi.org/10.1111/cdev.13988.

Cristea, Adrian, and Fotis Liarokapis. "Fractal Nature: Generating Realistic Terrains for Games." *IEEE Xplore* (2015). https://doi.org/10.1109/vs-games.2015.7295776.

Crutchfield, James P. "Between Order and Chaos." *Nature Physics* 8 (2012): 17–24. https://doi.org/10.1038/nphys2190.

Csernus, Valér, and Béla Mess. "Biorhythms and Pineal Gland." *Neuroendocrinology Letters* 24, no. 6 (2003): 404–411. https://pubmed.ncbi.nlm.nih.gov/15073565.

Dean, J. G. "Indolethylamine-N-methyltransferase Polymorphisms: Genetic and Biochemical Approaches for Study of Endogenous N,N,-dimethyltryptamine." *Frontiers in Neuroscience* 12 (2018). https://doi.org/10.3389/fnins.2018.00232.

Dean, J. G., T. Liu, Sean Huff, et al. "Biosynthesis and Extracellular Concentrations of N,N-dimethyltryptamine (DMT) in Mammalian Brain." *Scientific Reports* 9 (2019). https://doi.org/10.1038/s41598-019-45812-w.

Deepeshwar, Singh, Suhas A. Vinchurkar, Naveen K. Visweswaraiah, and Hongasandra R. Nagendra. "Hemodynamic Responses on Prefrontal Cortex Related to Meditation and Attentional Task." *Frontiers in Systems Neuroscience* 8 (2015). https://doi.org/10.3389/fnsys.2014.00252.

Dispenza, Joe. *Breaking the Habit of Being Yourself: How to Lose Your Mind and Create a New One*. Hay House, 2013.

Domhoff, G. W. "The Dreams of Men and Women: Patterns of Gender Similarity and Difference." University of California, Santa Cruz, 2005. https://dreams.ucsc.edu/Library/domhoff_2005c.html.

Dunlap Jr., Orrin E. "An Inventor's Seasoned Ideas." *The New York Times*, April 8, 1934. https://teslauniverse.com/nikola-tesla/articles/tesla-sees-evidence-radio-and-light-are-sound.

Einstein, Albert. Quoted in Evelyn Fox Keller, *A Feeling for the Organism: The Life and Work of Barbara McClintock*. W.H. Freeman, 1983.

Fell, Juergen, Nikolai Axmacher, and Sven Haupt. "From Alpha to Gamma: Electrophysiological Correlates of Meditation-Related States of Consciousness." *Medical Hypotheses* 75, no. 2 (2010): 218–224. https://doi.org/10.1016/j.mehy.2010.02.025.

Freye, Enno. "Dimethyltryptamine (DMT) a Psychedelic." In *Pharmacology and Abuse of Cocaine, Amphetamines, Ecstasy and Related Designer Drugs*. Springer, 2009.

"Generation Z Expresses Concerns Regarding the Toxicity and Addictiveness of Social Media." Disinformation Social Media Alliance, April 17, 2025. https://disa.org/generation-z-expresses-concerns-regarding-the-toxicity-and-addictiveness-of-social-media.

Gopnik, Alison, Shaun O'Grady, Christopher G. Lucas, et al. "Changes in Cognitive Flexibility and Hypothesis Search across Human Life History from Childhood to Adolescence to Adulthood." *Proceedings of the National Academy of Sciences* 114, no. 30 (2017): 7892–7899. https://doi.org/10.1073/pnas.1700811114.

Grammenos, Dionysios, and Steven A. Barker. "On the Transmethylation Hypothesis: Stress, *N,N*-dimethyltryptamine, and Positive Symptoms of Psychosis." *Journal of Neural Transmission* 122 (2015): 733–739. https://doi.org/10.1007/s00702-014-1329-5.

Grieco, Steven F., Eero Castrén, Gitte M. Knudsen, et al. "Psychedelics and Neural Plasticity: Therapeutic Implications." *The Journal of Neuroscience* 42, no. 45 (2022): 8439–8449. https://doi.org/10.1523/jneurosci.1121-22.2022.

Grivas, Theodoros B., and Olga D. Savvidou. "Melatonin the 'Light of Night' in Human Biology and Adolescent Idiopathic Scoliosis." *Scoliosis* 2 (2007). https://doi.org/10.1186/1748-7161-2-6.

Grof, Stanislav. *Realms of the Human Unconscious: Observations from LSD Research*. Dutton, 1976.

Guendelman, Simón, Sebastián Medeiros, and Hagen Rampes. "Mindfulness and Emotion Regulation: Insights from

Neurobiological, Psychological, and Clinical Studies." *Frontiers in Psychology* 8 (2017). https://doi.org/10.3389/fpsyg.2017.00220.

Guo, Xiaoli, Meiyun Wang, Xu Wang, et al. "Progressive Increase of High-Frequency EEG Oscillations during Meditation Is Associated with Its Trait Effects on Heart Rate and Proteomics: A Study on the Tibetan Buddhist." *Cerebral Cortex* 32, no. 18 (2022): 3865–3877. https://doi.org/10.1093/cercor/bhab453.

Gu, X., P. R. Hof, K. J. Friston, and J. Fan. "Anterior Insular Cortex and Emotional Awareness." *Journal of Comparative Neurology* 521, no. 15 (2013): 3371–3388. https://doi.org/10.1002/cne.23368.

Hadjipapas, Avgis, C. Charalambous, and Mark J. Roberts. "Editorial: Why the Exact Frequencies in Our Brains Matter: Perspectives from Electrophysiology and Brain Stimulation." *Frontiers in Systems Neuroscience* 16 (2023). https://doi.org/10.3389/fnsys.2022.1121438.

Hägnevik, K., G. Faxelius, L. Irestedt, H. Lagercrantz, B. Lundell, and B. Persson. "Catecholamine Surge and Metabolic Adaptation in the Newborn After Vaginal Delivery and Caesarean Section." *Acta Paediatrica* 73, no. 5 (1984): 602–609. https://doi.org/10.1111/j.1651-2227.1984.tb09982.x.

HistoryofScience.com. "The Scope of Benoît Mandelbrot's Work and Its Influence." https://www.historyofscience.com/pdf/The%20Scope%20of%20Benoit%20Mandelbrot's%20Work%20and%20its%20Influence.pdf.

Hofmann, Albert. *LSD: My Problem Child*. Translated by Jonathan Ott. McGraw-Hill, 1980.

Intuitor.com. "Nikola Tesla (1856–1943): Master of Resonance." The Physics of Resonance. http://intuitor.com/resonance/tesla.php.

Jenny, Hans. *Cymatics: A Study of Wave Phenomena and Vibration*, vol. 1. MACROmedia Publishing, 2001.

Johansson, Pär Ingemar, Jakob Stensballe, Lars Simon Rasmussen, and Sisse Rye Ostrowski. "High Circulating Adrenaline Levels at

Admission Predict Increased Mortality After Trauma." *The Journal of Trauma and Acute Care Surgery* 72, no. 2 (2012): 428–436. https://doi.org/10.1097/ta.0b013e31821e0f93.

Jung, Carl G. *Memories, Dreams, Reflections*. Edited by Aniela Jaffé. Translated by Richard and Clara Winston. Pantheon Books, 1963.

Jung, Carl G. *The Collected Works of C. G. Jung, Volume 9 (Part I): The Archetypes and the Collective Unconscious*. Edited and translated by Gerhard Adler and R. F. C. Hull. Princeton University Press, 1969.

Jung, Carl G. "The Meaning of Psychology for Modern Man." In *The Quotable Jung*, edited by Judith R. Harris. Princeton University Press, 2016.

Karnick, Aleksandr T., Brian W. Bauer, and Daniel W. Capron. "Negative Mood and Optimism Bias: An Experimental Investigation of Sadness and Belief Updating." *Journal of Behavior Therapy and Experimental Psychiatry* 82 (2024): 101910. https://doi.org/10.1016/j.jbtep.2023.101910.

Khandare, A. L., G. S. Rao, and N. Lakshmaiah. "Effect of Tamarind Ingestion on Fluoride Excretion in Humans." *European Journal of Clinical Nutrition* 56 (2002): 82–85. https://doi.org/10.1038/sj.ejcn.1601287.

Kim, Minkyung, Hyoungkyu Kim, Zirui Huang, et al. "Criticality Creates a Functional Platform for Network Transitions Between Internal and External Processing Modes in the Human Brain." *Frontiers in Systems Neuroscience* 15 (2021). https://doi.org/10.3389/fnsys.2021.657809.

Kuhn, Robert Lawrence. "A Landscape of Consciousness: Toward a Taxonomy of Explanations and Implications." *Progress in Biophysics and Molecular Biology* 190 (2024): 28–169. https://doi.org/10.1016/j.pbiomolbio.2023.12.003.

Kuypers, K. P. C., J. Riba, M. de la Fuente Revenga, S. Barker, E. L. Theunissen, and J. G. Ramaekers. "Ayahuasca Enhances Creative

Divergent Thinking While Decreasing Conventional Convergent Thinking." *Psychopharmacology* 233 (2016): 3395–3403. https://doi.org/10.1007/s00213-016-4377-8.

Lardone, Anna, Marianna Liparoti, Pierpaolo Sorrentino, et al. "Mindfulness Meditation Is Related to Long-Lasting Changes in Hippocampal Functional Topology during Resting State: A Magnetoencephalography Study." *Neural Plasticity* (2018). https://doi.org/10.1155/2018/5340717.

Last, Nicole, Emily Tufts, and Leslie E. Auger. "The Effects of Meditation on Grey Matter Atrophy and Neurodegeneration: A Systematic Review." *Journal of Alzheimer's Disease* 56, no. 1 (2016): 275–286. https://doi.org/10.3233/jad-160899.

Lokhorst, Gert-Jan. "Descartes and the Pineal Gland." *The Stanford Encyclopedia of Philosophy* Winter 2021 Edition (2021). https://plato.stanford.edu/archives/win2021/entries/pineal-gland.

Luke, David. "Discarnate Entities and Dimethyltryptamine (DMT): Psychopharmacology, Phenomenology and Ontology." *Journal of the Society for Psychical Research* 75, no. 902 (2011): 26–42. https://docslib.org/doc/4959812/discarnate-entities-and-dimethyltryptamine-dmt-psychopharmacology-phenomenology-and-ontology.

Luke, Jennifer A. "The Effect of Fluoride on the Physiology of the Pineal Gland." PhD diss., University of Surrey, 1997. https://openresearch.surrey.ac.uk/esploro/outputs/doctoral/The-Effect-of-Fluoride-on-the/99516257402346.

Makin, A. D. J., M. Roccato, E. Karakashevska, J. Tyson-Carr, and M. Bertamini. "Symmetry Perception and Psychedelic Experience." *Symmetry* 15, no. 7 (2023): 1340. https://doi.org/10.3390/sym15071340.

Manske, Richard H. F. "A Synthesis of Methyltryptamines and Some Derivatives." *Canadian Journal of Research* 5, no. 5 (1931): 592–600. https://doi.org/10.1139/cjr31-097.

Marlo, Helen. "Precognitive Dreams: When Your Dreams Come True." *Psychology Today*, March 25, 2025. https://www.psychologytoday.com/gb/blog/deeper-dive/202503/precognitive-dreams-when-your-dreams-come-true?msockid=399532b88aff6a7d3c1c242a8bf36b11.

Mason, Natasha L., Elisabeth Mischler, Malin V. Uthaug, and K. P. C. Kuypers. "Sub-Acute Effects of Psilocybin on Empathy, Creative Thinking, and Subjective Well-Being." *Journal of Psychoactive Drugs* 51, no. 2 (2019): 123–134. https://doi.org/10.1080/02791072.2019.1580804.

Maurer, Daphne, Thanujeni Pathman, and Catherine J. Mondloch. "The Shape of Boubas: Sound-Shape Correspondences in Toddlers and Adults." *Developmental Science* 9, no. 3 (2006): 316–322. https://doi.org/10.1111/j.1467-7687.2006.00495.x.

Maxwell, Richard W., and Sucharit Katyal. "Characteristics of Kundalini-Related Sensory, Motor, and Affective Experiences During Tantric Yoga Meditation." *Frontiers in Psychology* 13 (2022). https://doi.org/10.3389/fpsyg.2022.863091.

McKenna, Terence. *Food of the Gods: The Search for the Original Tree of Knowledge*. Bantam, 1993.

McKenna, Terence. "Terence McKenna on Fractals." Posted August 17, 2021, by We Plants Are Happy Plants. YouTube, 25 min., 27 sec. https://www.youtube.com/watch?v=qWKCsrwA1PY.

McKenna, Terence. *True Hallucinations: Being an Account of the Author's Extraordinary Adventures in the Devil's Paradise*. HarperOne, 1994.

Meshkat, Shakila, T. J. Tello-Gerez, Fatemeh Gholaminezhad, et al. "Impact of Psilocybin on Cognitive Function: A Systematic Review." *Psychiatry and Clinical Neurosciences* 78, no. 12 (2024): 744–764. https://doi.org/10.1111/pcn.13741.

Miller, John J., Ken Fletcher, and Jon Kabat-Zinn. "Three-Year Follow-Up and Clinical Implications of a Mindfulness Meditation-Based Stress Reduction Intervention in the Treatment of Anxiety

Disorders." *General Hospital Psychiatry* 17, no. 3 (1995): 192–200. https://doi.org/10.1016/0163-8343(95)00025-M.

Moujaes, F., N. M. Rieser, L. Belinger, M. Herdener, Z. Zahid, and K. H. Preller. "The Emotional Architecture of the Psychedelic Brain." *Trends in Cognitive Sciences* 29, no. 11 (2025): 1007–1022. https://doi.org/10.1016/j.tics.2025.07.006.

Mrazek, Michael D., Michael S. Franklin, Dawa T. Phillips, Benjamin Baird, and Jonathan W. Schooler. "Mindfulness Training Improves Working Memory Capacity and GRE Performance While Reducing Mind Wandering." *Psychological Science* 24, no. 5 (2013): 776–781. https://doi.org/10.1177/0956797612459659.

Muraresku, Brian C. *The Immortality Key: The Secret History of the Religion with No Name.* St. Martin's Press, 2020.

Muthukumaraswamy, Suresh. "High-Frequency Brain Activity and Muscle Artifacts in MEG/EEG: A Review and Recommendations." *Frontiers in Human Neuroscience* 7 (2013). https://doi.org/10.3389/fnhum.2013.00138.

Naddaf, Miryam. "How Your Brain Detects Patterns in the Everyday: Without Conscious Thought." *Nature*, September 25, 2024. https://www.nature.com/articles/d41586-024-03116-8.

National Center for Complementary and Integrative Health. "Melatonin: What You Need to Know." Last modified May 2024. https://www.nccih.nih.gov/health/melatonin-what-you-need-to-know.

"Near-Death Experiences," *Psychology Today*. https://www.psychologytoday.com/us/basics/near-death-experiences?msockid=399532b88aff6a7d3c1c242a8bf36b11.

Nichols, David E. "Psychedelics." *Pharmacological Reviews* 68, no. 2 (2016): 264–355. https://doi.org/10.1124/pr.115.011478.

Nicholson, Reynold A. *The Mathnawí of Jalálu'ddín Rúmí.* Messrs. Luzac & Co., 1926.

Nietzsche, Friedrich. *Thus Spoke Zarathustra*. Translated by Walter Kaufmann. Modern Library, 1995.

Nietzsche, Friedrich. "Why I Am So Clever." In *Ecce Homo: How One Becomes What One Is*, translated by R. J. Hollingdale. Insel-Verlag, 1908.

Nørretranders, Tor. *The User Illusion: Cutting Consciousness Down to Size*. Penguin Books, 1999.

Olami, Amit, and Leehe Peled-Avron. "Effects of Classical Psychedelics on Implicit and Explicit Emotional Empathy and Cognitive Empathy: A Meta-Analysis of MET Task." *Scientific Reports* 14 (2024). https://doi.org/10.1038/s41598-024-74810-w.

Palahniuk, Chuck. *Survivor*. W. W. Norton, 1999.

Plath, Sylvia. *The Bell Jar*. Harper & Row, 1971.

Reiter, Russel J., R. Sharma, S. Rosales-Corral, et al. "Melatonin in Ventricular and Subarachnoid Cerebrospinal Fluid: Its Function in the Neural Glymphatic Network and Biological Significance for Neurocognitive Health." *Biochemical and Biophysical Research Communications* 605 (2022): 70–81. https://doi.org/10.1016/j.bbrc.2022.03.025.

Robson, David. "Blindsight: The Strangest Form of Consciousness." *BBC*, September 28, 2015. https://www.bbc.com/future/article/20150925-blindsight-the-strangest-form-of-consciousness.

Sadhguru, host. *Sadhguru's Podcast*. Podcast transcription. "Something Phenomenal Happens at 3:40 AM: Brahma Muhurtam." https://podcasts.happyscribe.com/sadhguru-s-podcast/something-phenomenal-happens-at-3-40-am-sadhguru-brahma-muhurtam.

Samorini, Giorgio. "The Oldest Archeological Data Evidencing the Relationship of *Homo sapiens* with Psychoactive Plants: A Worldwide Overview." *Journal of Psychedelic Studies* 3, no. 2 (2019): 63–80. https://doi.org/10.1556/2054.2019.008.

Schredl, Michael, and Iris Reinhard. "Gender Differences in Dream Recall: A Meta–Analysis." *Journal of Sleep Research* 17, no. 2 (2008): 125–131. https://doi.org/10.1111/j.1365-2869.2008.00626.x.

Shonkoff, Jack P., et al. "Children's Emotional Development Is Built into the Architecture of Their Brains." Working Paper No. 2. Center on the Developing Child, Harvard University, August 2011. https://harvardcenter.wpenginepowered.com/wp-content/uploads/2004/04/Childrens-Emotional-Development-Is-Built-into-the-Architecture-of-Their-Brains.pdf.

Shonle, Ruth. "Peyote, the Giver of Visions." *American Anthropologist* 27, no. 1 (1925): 53–75. https://www.jstor.org/stable/661497.

Sinek, Simon. "Love Your Work." Hosted by Tina Roth Eisenberg. Posted April 20, 2012, by CreativeMornings. Video, 42 min., 8 sec. https://creativemornings.com/talks/simon-sinek.

Skene, Debra J., and Josephine Arendt. "Circadian Rhythm Sleep Disorders in the Blind and Their Treatment with Melatonin." *Sleep Medicine* 8, no. 6 (2007): 651–655. https://doi.org/10.1016/j.sleep.2006.11.013.

"So-Called Indigo Teen Says She Can Read People." ABC News, July 25, 2006. https://abcnews.go.com/GMA/AmericanFamily/story?id=2224795&page=1.

Sound of Creation, season 1, episode 1, "Sacred Secrets of Sound," featuring Gregg Braden, released 2022, on Gaia, https://www.gaia.com/video/sacred-secrets-of-sound.

Spencer, Herta, Isaac Lewin, Josephine Fowler, and Joseph Samachson. "Effect of Sodium Fluoride on Calcium Absorption and Balances in Man." *The American Journal of Clinical Nutrition* 22, no. 4 (1969): 381–390. https://doi.org/10.1093/ajcn/22.4.381.

Stanton, Sarah Dyanne. "Intuition: A Silver Lining for Clinicians with Complex Trauma." Master's thesis, Syracuse University, 2016. https://surface.syr.edu/etd/615.

Stewart, Omer C. *Peyote Religion: A History*. University of Oklahoma Press, 1993.

Strassman, Rick. *DMT: The Spirit Molecule: A Doctor's Revolutionary Research into the Biology of Near-Death and Mystical Experiences*. Park Street Press, 2001.

Strassman, Rick J., Glenn T. Peake, Clifford R. Qualls, and E. Jonathan Lisansky. "A Model for the Study of the Acute Effects of Melatonin in Man." *Journal of Clinical Endocrinology & Metabolism* 65, no. 5 (1987): 847–852. https://doi.org/10.1210/jcem-65-5-847.

Sumida, M., A. J. Barkovich, and T. H. Newton. "Development of the Pineal Gland: Measurement with MR." *American Journal of Neuroradiology* 17, no. 2 (1996): 233–236. https://www.ajnr.org/content/17/2/233.short.

Sweeney, Mary M., S. Nayak, E. S. Hurwitz, L. N. Mitchell, T. C. Swift, and R. R. Griffiths. "Comparison of Psychedelic and Near-Death or Other Non-Ordinary Experiences in Changing Attitudes About Death and Dying." *PLOS One* 17, no. 8 (2022): e0271926. https://doi.org/10.1371/journal.pone.0271926.

Tan, Dun X., Bing Xu, Xinjia Zhou, and Russel J. Reiter. "Pineal Calcification, Melatonin Production, Aging, Associated Health Consequences and Rejuvenation of the Pineal Gland." *Molecules* 23, no. 2 (2018): 301. https://doi.org/10.3390/molecules23020301.

Tang, Yi-Yuan, Britta K. Hölzel, and Michael I. Posner. "The Neuroscience of Mindfulness Meditation." *Nature Reviews Neuroscience* 16 (2015): 213–225. https://doi.org/10.1038/nrn3916.

Tesla, Nikola. *My Inventions: The Autobiography of Nikola Tesla*. Electrical Experimenter, 1919.

The NDE. "Pam Reynolds Near Death Experience." https://www.neardth.com/pam-reynolds-nde.php.

"The Neuroscience of Creativity and 'Aha!' Moments." *Science News Today*, August 8, 2025. https://www.sciencenewstoday.org/the-neuroscience-of-creativity-and-aha-moments.

The Personal Site of Lalo Morales. "Nikola Tesla's Resonance Theories and the Schumann Resonance: An In-Depth Review." https://www.laloadrianmorales.com/blog/nikola-teslas-resonance-theories-and-the-schumann-resonance-an-in-depth-review.

"The Renaissance: The Age of Michelangelo and Leonardo Da Vinci (1/2)." Posted April 28, 2019, by DW Documentary. YouTube, 42 min., 25 sec. https://www.youtube.com/watch?v=BmHTQsxxkPk.

The Three Initiates. *The Kybalion: A Study of the Hermetic Philosophy of Ancient Egypt and Greece.* Yogi Publication Society, 1908.

Tian, Yang, Zeren Tan, Hedong Hou, et al. "Theoretical Foundations of Studying Criticality in the Brain." *Network Neuroscience* 6, no. 4 (2022): 1148–1185. https://doi.org/10.1162/netn_a_00269.

Vidafar, Parisa, Elise M. McGlashan, Angus C. Burns, et al. "Greater Sensitivity of the Circadian System of Women to Bright Light, but Not Dim–to–Moderate Light." *Journal of Pineal Research* 76, no. 2 (2024): e12936. https://doi.org/10.1111/jpi.12936.

Voss, Ursula, and Allan Hobson. "What Is the State-of-the-Art on Lucid Dreaming? Recent Advances and Questions for Future Research." In *Open MIND*, edited by Thomas Metzinger and Jennifer M. Windt. MIT Press, 2015.

Voss, Ursula, Clemens Frenzel, Judith Koppehele-Gossel, and Allan Hobson. "Lucid Dreaming: An Age-Dependent Brain Dissociation." *Journal of Sleep Research* 21, no. 6 (2012): 634–642. https://doi.org/10.1111/j.1365-2869.2012.01022.x.

Watts, Alan W. *The Way of Zen.* Pantheon Books, 1957.

Watts, Alan W. *The Wisdom of Insecurity: A Message for an Age of Anxiety.* Pantheon Books, 1951.

Werrett, Anna. "The Effects of Melatonin on Testosterone Levels: What You Need to Know." MedShun, January 21, 2024. https://medshun.com/article/does-melatonin-affect-testosterone.

Westerhoff, Jan. "Reality: Is Matter Real?" *New Scientist*, September 26, 2012. https://www.newscientist.com/article/mg21528840-700-reality-is-matter-real.

"What to Know About Calcification of the Pineal Gland." *WebMD*, October 16, 2024. https://www.webmd.com/sleep-disorders/what-to-know-about-calcification-of-the-pineal-gland.

"What to Know About Gamma Brain Waves." *WebMD*, October 1, 2025. https://www.webmd.com/brain/what-to-know-about-gamma-brain-waves.

Wießner, Isabel, Marcelo Falchi, Lucas Oliveira Maia, et al. "LSD and Creativity: Increased Novelty and Symbolic Thinking, Decreased Utility and Convergent Thinking." *Journal of Psychopharmacology* 36, no. 3 (2022). https://doi.org/10.1177/02698811211069113.

Wolff, Tom John. "Research About DMT and Ayahuasca." In *The Touristic Use of Ayahuasca in Peru: Expectations, Experiences, Meanings and Subjective Effects*. Springer VS Wiesbaden, 2020.

Woolfe, Sam. "How to Integrate a Difficult-to-Remember DMT Experience." Maps of the Mind, March 9, 2020. https://mapsofthemind.com/2020/09/03/how-to-integrate-difficult-remember-dmt-experience/#:~:text=One%20of%20the%20most%20common%20features%20%28and%20frustrations%29,trip%20as%20you%20return%20to%20normal%20waking%20consciousness.

Wurtman, Richard J., and Julius Axelrod. "The Pineal Gland." *Scientific American* 213, no. 1 (1965): 50–63. https://www.jstor.org/stable/24931939.

Acknowledgments

This book would not have been possible without the support of countless friends, family members, and mentors who believed in me. To my wonderful conscious community for giving me a voice, and to my publisher and talented editors for taking a chance on me: thank you from the heart.

About the Author

Misia Welters is a UK-based meditation teacher and intuition specialist. She is dedicated to guiding others toward deeper self-awareness and spiritual empowerment. With a lifelong practice that began at the age of twelve, she now works full-time providing intuitive guidance and meditation coaching. Misia engages with a vibrant online audience of over half a million followers across Instagram, TikTok, and her blog, where she explores the meeting point between ancient philosophy, metaphysics, and contemporary science. Through her writing and coaching, she offers practical pathways to inner wisdom, self-discovery, and meaningful personal transformation.

Key Lime Publishing is an independent publisher founded by former members of the award-winning Mango Publishing team. Collectively, we've published more than 1,000 books since 2014, selling over 10 million copies and earning national recognition along the way. Now, we're channeling that experience into reimagining what publishing can be in a rapidly changing world.

Our mission is simple yet ambitious: to empower new and underrepresented authors, connecting their voices with readers in authentic, meaningful ways, while staying agile in the face of the challenges reshaping the publishing industry. From the rise of AI to shifting global supply chains, inflationary pressures, and industry uncertainty, the landscape of 2026 and beyond demands resilience, creativity, and bold new strategies.

That's why Key Lime is harnessing the experience of building one of fastest-growing independent publishers in the US over the last decade to create a publishing house tailored to modern authors looking to connect with their audience and new readers.

Please stay in touch with us and follow us on our website (keylimepublishing.com) and Instagram (@KeyLimePublishing).

Thanks for reading!

www.ingramcontent.com/pod-product-compliance
Lightning Source LLC
Chambersburg PA
CBHW011550070526
44585CB00023B/2523